SOCIAL WORK

Series Editor: Jo Campling

BASW

Editorial Advisory Board:
Robert Adams, Terry Bamford, Charles Barker,
Lena Dominelli, Malcolm Payne, Michael Preston-Shoot,
Daphne Statham and Jane Tunstill

Social work is at an important stage in its development. All professions must be responsive to changing social and economic conditions if they are to meet the needs of those they serve. This series focuses on sound practice and the specific contribution which social workers can make to the well-being of our society.

The British Association of Social Workers has always been conscious of its role in setting guidelines for practice and in seeking to raise professional standards. The conception of the Practical Social Work series arose from a survey of BASW members to discover where they, the practitioners in social work, felt there was the most need for new literature. The response was overwhelming and enthusiastic, and the result is a carefully planned, coherent series of books. The emphasis is firmly on practice, set in a theoretical framework. The books will inform, stimulate and promote discussion, thus adding to the further development of skills and high professional standards. All the authors are practitioners and/or teachers of social work representing a wide variety of experience.

JO CAMPLING

A list of published titles in this series follows overleaf

**Practical Social Work
Series Standing Order ISBN 0–333–69347–7**

You can receive future titles in this series as they are published by placing a standing order. Please contact your bookseller or, in the case of difficulty, write to us at the address below with your name and address, the title of the series and the ISBN quoted above.

Customer Services Department, Macmillan Distribution Ltd
Houndmills, Basingstoke, Hampshire RG21 6XS, England

PRACTICAL SOCIAL WORK

Robert Adams *Social Work and Empowerment*

Sarah Banks *Ethics and Values in Social Work (2nd edn)*

James G. Barber *Beyond Casework*

James G. Barber *Social Work with Addictions*

Peter Beresford and Suzy Croft *Citizen Involvement*

Suzy Braye and Michael Preston-Shoot *Practising Social Work Law (2nd edn)*

Helen Cosis Brown *Social Work and Sexuality*

Alan Butler and Colin Pritchard *Social Work and Mental Illness*

Crescy Cannan, Lynne Berry and Karen Lyons *Social Work and Europe*

Roger Clough *Residential Work*

David M. Cooper and David Ball *Social Work and Child Abuse*

Veronica Coulshed and Audrey Mullender *Management in Social Work (2nd edn)*

Veronica Coulshed and Joan Orme *Social Work Practice: An Introduction (3rd edn)*

Paul Daniel and John Wheeler *Social Work and Local Politics*

Peter R. Day *Sociology in Social Work Practice*

Lena Dominelli *Anti-Racist Social Work (2nd edn)*

Celia Doyle *Working with Abused Children (2nd edn)*

Angela Everitt and Pauline Hardiker *Evaluating for Good Practice*

Angela Everitt, Pauline Hardiker, Jane Littlewood and Audrey Mullender *Applied Research for Better Practice*

Kathy Ford and Alan Jones *Student Supervision*

David Francis and Paul Henderson *Working with Rural Communities*

Alison Froggatt *Family Work with Elderly People*

Danya Glaser and Stephen Frosh *Child Sexual Abuse (2nd edn)*

Gill Gorell Barnes *Working with Families*

Cordelia Grimwood and Ruth Popplestone *Women, Management and Care*

Jalna Hanmer and Daphne Statham *Women and Social Work*

Tony Jeffs and Mark Smith (eds) *Youth Work*

Michael Kerfoot and Alan Butler *Problems of Childhood and Adolescence*

Joyce Lishman *Communication in Social Work*

Carol Lupton and Terry Gillespie (eds) *Working with Violence*

Mary Marshall and Mary Dixon *Social Work with Older People (3rd edn)*

Paula Nicolson and Rowan Bayne *Applied Psychology for Social Workers (2nd edn)*

Kieran O'Hagan *Crisis Intervention in Social Services*

Michael Oliver and Bob Sapey *Social Work with Disabled People (2nd edn)*

Joan Orme and Bryan Glastonbury *Care Management*

John Pitts *Working with Young Offenders (2nd edn)*

Michael Preston-Shoot *Effective Groupwork*

Peter Raynor, David Smith and Maurice Vanstone *Effective Probation Practice*

Steven Shardlow and Mark Doel *Practice Learning and Teaching*

Carole R. Smith *Social Work with the Dying and Bereaved*

David Smith *Criminology for Social Work*

Christine Stones *Focus on Families*

Neil Thompson *Anti-Discriminatory Practice (3rd edn)*

Neil Thompson, Michael Murphy and Steve Stradling *Dealing with Stress*

Derek Tilbury *Working with Mental Illness*

Alan Twelvetrees *Community Work (3rd edn)*

Hilary Walker and Bill Beaumont (eds) *Working with Offenders*

Community Work

Third Edition

Alan Twelvetrees

 in association with

COMMUNITY
DEVELOPMENT
FOUNDATION

First edition 1982
Reprinted four times
Second edition 1991
Reprinted eight times
Third edition 2002

Published by
PALGRAVE
Houndmills, Basingstoke, Hampshire RG21 6XS and
175 Fifth Avenue, New York, N.Y. 10010
Companies and representatives throughout the world

PALGRAVE is the new global academic imprint of St. Martin's Press LLC Scholarly and Reference Division and Palgrave Publishers Ltd (formerly Macmillan Press Ltd).

ISBN 0–333–91270–5

This book is printed on paper suitable for recycling and made from fully managed and sustained forest sources.

A catalogue record for this book is available from the British Library.

10   9   8   7   6   5   4   3
11   10   09   08   07   06   05   04   03

Printed in China

Contents

Preface

Writing a book about community work is a bit like painting the Forth bridge (near Edinburgh, Scotland); as soon as you have finished, it needs doing again. While the principles of practice I described in the earlier editions of this book still hold broadly true, the contexts of practice have, in some cases, shifted markedly. For instance, in the 1970s, community work, in Britain, at least, was closely associated with social work. Today, it seems to link more with economic regeneration and planning. By the end of the 1980s the 'community enterprise' movement was very much on the scene in Britain, a movement which had scarcely been thought of a decade earlier. Additionally, many service agencies, concerned with health, social housing, the environment or crime prevention, for instance, were seeking to involve the community much more in designing and evaluating services.

Also, what I described as the 'radical tradition' of community work in the last edition of the book does not exist in any separate sense today (if it ever did). Rather, those who could be said to belong to that tradition might now be working 'for the state' (rather than seeking to work against it) in equal opportunities or related work, for instance.

For all these reasons, while there are perhaps fewer people designated as community workers today, their skills, and the values underlying these, are perhaps more widely required in a range of settings.

In Britain, the importance of ideas such as community involvement and consultation, empowerment and capacity building (whatever we mean by these) is now quite widely acknowledged. However, approaches consistent with these ideas have not often been integral to public policy initiatives, but peripheral and poorly thought through.

Nevertheless, it is coming to be recognised in many quarters for a range of different reasons that well organised, 'healthy' communities not only make a major contribution to the quality of life of their members but facilitate the delivery of other services which would not be so effective if the community was not organised.

The purpose of this edition, therefore, is to include information about these new contexts in which community work is practised and to give pointers, primarily to field level workers (but also to those funding or managing community work), about how to operate in them, as well as to include most of the 'how to do it' guidance which comprised the earlier editions.

The other changes are, of course, in me, the writer. I wrote the first edition of this book in my thirties after being a field level practitioner. While that edition contained some academic references, it was based primarily on my fieldwork experience. The second edition, which was published just after a thirteen-year spell teaching community work and doing research into it, inevitably drew more on 'theory' (both from Britain and abroad) as well as on the practice of my students.

Since 1989 I have been working again in the field but for a national organisation which exists to promote community work (the Community Development Foundation). This time, however, I have set up projects, managed staff, liaised at a fairly high level with central and local governments, politicians and, to a lesser extent, businesses in order to win resources for and encourage others to invest in community development programmes. I have also learned a little, through visits, about aspects of community work in some other countries. Increasingly, I believe that, while the contexts are different, the 'universals' are the same, and I am now conscious that what I write may have relevance to other countries besides the UK. For that reason I have tried to emphasise these 'universal' issues rather than the specific organisational and legislative contexts which apply in Britain alone. I also believe that the values and skills of community work will be required in many countries for the forseeable future and that community work is thus, in a sense, an idea for all time.

I can only tell you, the reader, what community work is for me and hope you find my thoughts relevant to your situation. If the book does not speak to your experience or if you have had other experiences which are not included in it, please let me know.

My thanks go to many more people than I can name: to those who have disagreed with me, for instance, because they have forced me to think through my ideas; to those whose love and respect has encouraged me to believe I have something useful to say; to all those people who have in some way taught me something;

and of course, to the many people who have helped directly and indirectly with the book, Gwyneth Goodhead my typist, Tom Bell, Steve Forster, Steve Skinner, Jenny Sayer, Ruth Marks, Peter Hirst, Tony Kelly, Cormack McAleer, Pamela Coates, Paul Henderson, Christiane Forêt, Gilbert Dif, Hally Ingram, Alison Gilchrist, Sue King, Stuart Hashagen, Chris Owen, Lydia Merill, Susan Hodgett, Robert Cornwall, Charlie Garratt, Susan Allen, Nia Higginbotham, Carol Green, Anna Freeman, Ciaran Traynor, Oliver Twelvetrees and Catherine Mackereth.

ALAN TWELVETREES

1

What Is Community Work?

Introduction

Many kinds of spontaneous and autonomous initiatives arise in communities run by the members of those communities. This book is not about such initiatives themselves but, rather, about the process of assisting and supporting them, essentially by another organisation or worker. Thus, at its simplest, community work is *the process of assisting people to improve their own communities by undertaking collective action.* The provision of this assistance generally requires the employment of paid workers, and it is their work which is the main focus of this book. I will call such people 'community workers'. However, unpaid community leaders (and indeed others) might also call themselves community workers even though their main role was not to offer support to autonomous community initiatives.

These paid workers are employed in a number of different guises and may be called voluntary services officers, liaison officers, development workers, and the like. They may undertake a wide range of functions, as a result of which community work takes a great variety of forms (which may sometimes not be easy to distinguish either from the spontaneous community initiatives described above or from the delivery of services in a way that involves the community). Community work may also be carried out by a range of service professionals – social workers, housing officers or health workers, for example – as an addition to their 'normal' work.

The essence of community work is to ensure, first, that people, as residents of geographical communities or as members of high need groups (such as people with learning difficulties) get a better deal;

and second, that they bring this 'better deal' about themselves, at least as far as possible, and develop more skills and confidence in the process.

The main rationale for employing staff to facilitate the development of such groups is twofold. First, a progressive and healthy society needs the active participation of its citizens in a wide variety of ways. Urban renewal tends to fail, for instance, when it is undertaken over the heads of local people. Citizen participation is also vital, in my view, as a means of holding politicians and policy-makers to account. Secondly, without assistance, many attempts of people to engage in collective action and other forms of participation fail, especially in 'excluded' communities.

Therefore, ways need to be found of working to create, support and strengthen community groups and to ensure that they are effective, inclusive, democratic and work for just ends. Thus, the main tasks of a community worker on, say, a disadvantaged housing estate, might be to help people set up and run, usually on a voluntary basis, tenants' associations, youth groups, senior citizens organisations and so on.

However, community workers undertake many other activities besides offering support to community groups. There are in fact a number of different approaches to the work and it is important to try to categorise them. It needs saying, however, that the messy reality of practice only approximates in general terms to these 'ideal types'. They serve to enhance our understanding of community work; they do not describe it exactly.

Each category is listed below in the form of a bipolar continuum. I then go on to explain them.

- Community development approaches as opposed to social planning approaches.
- Self-help or service approaches as opposed to influence approaches.
- Generic community work as opposed to specialist community work.
- Concern about 'process' as opposed to concern about 'product'.
- The enabling as opposed to the organising role of the worker.
- Community work in its own right as opposed to an approach or attitude in other forms of work.

- Unpaid community work as opposed to paid community work.

Community development approaches and social planning approaches

If we look at community workers who work in small neighbourhoods, we find that they usually operate in two main ways. The first way is, as indicated, to assist existing groups or help people form new autonomous groups. This approach can most usefully be called the *community development approach*, and it is this form of work which is most unique to community work. In its 'pure' form the community development approach emphasises the objectivity of workers and implies they will work 'non-directively' with people on what *they* decide to become involved with, whether it is running a playgroup or campaigning for better services.

The second main way in which a worker operates is liaising and working directly with policy-makers and service providers to sensitise them to the needs of specific communities and to assist them to improve services or alter policies. I refer to this form of community work as the *social planning approach* although other phrases are sometimes used: 'inter-agency work' and, more recently, 'programme bending', for instance.

While, in my view, all community workers need to be able to work in both kinds of ways, some community work jobs will involve more opportunities for community development and others more opportunities for social planning. Inevitably, in a community work team some staff will primarily be doing community development work and others, especially the team leader, social planning.

There are also many forms of community work which involve both community development and social planning. For instance, an 'umbrella' organisation for a neighbourhood may consist of representatives both from community groups and, say, the local authority. Thus, a community worker who was servicing this group would be involved not only in community development but also in social planning as he or she would be working with both local people and service providers. Similarly, a community worker employed in a housing department to involve public sector tenants in housing policy would inevitably also do a great deal of work with policy makers.

Self help/service approaches and influence approaches

If we examine the role of the community group or organisation with which the worker is working, we note that some community needs can be met largely from the resources existing within the community – social events, play-schemes, voluntary youth clubs, lunch clubs for older people or disabled people, voluntary visiting schemes, women's groups, alcoholics anonymous groups, festivals, for instance. In these types of situations the group is involved in a self help or 'service' approach.

Other needs can only be met by modifying or changing the policies of organisations outside the community or by accessing resources from them. These kinds of needs require 'influence' approaches, which can involve everything from consensual work, such as applying for grants, 'working the system' and collaboration to campaigning, 'contest' and civil disobedience. Depending on the situation, a community worker is likely to be working at the same time with some groups on self help/service strategies and with (and for) others on influence approaches.

Generic community work and specialist community work

Some community workers are able to work on any issue – play, employment, leisure, housing and so on – and with any group – older people, women, disabled people, for instance – whatever kind of agency they work for. Such workers can be called generic workers. Because they do not have responsibility to deliver a particular service they are relatively free to work from the 'bottom up' in helping people articulate their needs and to come together to see that these are met.

However, funding agencies which are prepared to support generic 'bottom up' community work are difficult to find. On the other hand, many service agencies now recognise that in order to improve services to clients or consumers they have to involve them in the development of the service.

These service agencies are increasingly appointing *specialist* community workers (though they would usually have other job titles) whose jobs are, first, to extend and improve services and secondly to involve the consumers, often at a minimal level, in this process.

Thus, over the last two decades in Britain there has been a growing emphasis on what can be called specialist community work by service agencies either with the whole geographical community on a particular issue (for example, health) or with a specific category of people (people with learning difficulties, perhaps). Such workers are usually only able to work on the specific issues or with the population group with which the agency is concerned rather than to do generic community work. One implication of the development of this specialist work is that the worker is generally an expert on health or economic development or the needs of disabled people, for example, which is certainly necessary, but may lack community development skills.

While this specialist community work could, in theory, be primarily 'bottom up' (community development work), it is often centred on the needs of agencies for particular outcomes rather than on the needs of the community as articulated by its members. Thus, it tends to be 'top down' work (social planning) with only small amounts of 'bottom up' work.

As Willmott (1989) points out, 'top down' initiatives to involve the community can only work if 'bottom up' initiatives also exist. However, the paradox is that adequate resources are not usually devoted, by statutory agencies at least, to promoting 'bottom up' initiatives. Willmott concluded a decade ago that such top down (specialist) community initiatives are often ill thought out, under-resourced, under-evaluated and sometimes of doubtful value.

Process and product

Process goals are to do with changes in people's confidence, knowledge, technical skills or attitudes, or the development of an organisation. Product goals are to do with the changed material situation – an improved housing maintenance programme or a successful play scheme. Both kinds of goals are important throughout community work and they are intertwined.

Different situations tend to dictate whether process goals or product goals predominate. I was once working with a group to try to prevent a motorway from being built. In order to present evidence at the public enquiry a great deal of co-ordinated work had to be undertaken quickly. If process goals had predominated and

attention had been given to ensuring that the group members developed the skills to run this kind of campaign the deadline would
have been missed.

Community work is based on the central idea that product goals
should be brought about by a process which ensures that the participants in the action (community members) have as much control
as possible over all its aspects and that they acquire an enduring
capacity to act themselves (individually and collectively) as a result.
However, this process usually only works if product goals are also
met, since group members lose heart if they fail to achieve their
objectives. Therefore, in most situations workers have to give attention to both kinds of goals.

Some community groups are only concerned with process, and
these are sometimes called 'expressive' groups. They include educational, social, recreational and support groups, where the sole purpose of the group is the shared experience, the learning and other
social benefits within it. Expressive groups can be contrasted with
'instrumental groups' in which the main purpose is to organise
some collective action outside the group, running a newsletter, for
example.

While all groups have expressive functions, in that the members
gain or fail to gain from the social interaction in a meeting, some
groups have virtually no instrumental functions. It is important for
a worker to understand the main function of a group, since an
instrumental group needs members who can run meetings and organise action (that is, leaders) at least as well as people who could obtain
some benefit from being members but who might not contribute
towards product goals. If a worker is working with an instrumental
group, it is vital that he or she recruits (at least potential) community
leaders who are prepared to take (instrumental) action.

The enabling role and the organising role

The classic community work role is that of enabler, guide, catalyst
or facilitator where the worker goes at the pace of the group and
advises its members how to do what they want to do. This style of
work is also sometimes called 'non-directive'. However, there are
times when the worker may take a more directive, leadership or
organising role within a group, either informally or even as the chair

or secretary, usually because product goals need to predominate and because the group members may lack the necessary motivation or skills, at least at a particular time. In practice, the worker may move from less to more directive roles (or vice versa) and back again several times in one meeting.

Workers sometimes take on a wide range of other roles too: broker, advocate, 'fixer', trouble-shooter' and expert, for instance. The important point here is that workers need to be clear about what role they are playing at a particular time.

Community work in its own right and community work as an attitude or approach

When a worker is facilitating autonomous collective action in the community as his or her main job (or part of it) either as a generic or specialist worker, this can be called community work 'in its own right'. However, schoolteachers, postmen and women, local shopkeepers, community centre caretakers and many other paid employees, though not community workers, may carry out their work 'in a community work way'. That is, they show respect to community members, seek to learn from them, try to take their concerns into account when doing their own jobs, offer occasional advice or help to community leaders, and so on.

Thus, the central ideas which are to do with empowering individuals and groups, understanding the needs of others and taking these into account when actions are taken or policy is made, are not unique to community work. Indeed, good management, industrial relations, relations between family members, and relations between professionals and consumers reflect this ethos.

Unpaid and paid community work

There is no monopoly on the term 'community work'. For instance, many people who are active in their own communities, elected representatives, or committee members of voluntary organisations often claim to be community workers though they are unpaid. The main difference between paid and unpaid community work is, however, that the unpaid workers are usually leaders rather than facilitators. That difference distinguishes, on the whole, paid from unpaid community work and again emphasises the core (paid) community work role of being a facilitator.

An increasingly common way of looking at all this is to use 'community development' to describe the autonomous process by which community groups form and grow and to use community development *work* to describe the professional activity of supporting this process.

Starting where people are: a paradox

Two community workers on a council housing estate were keen to set up a tenants' association to pressurise the council to repair the housing more effectively. Tenants seemed interested and agreed to come to a meeting to discuss it. Nobody came. The workers organised two other meetings and the total attendance was one person. Then, some tenants asked the workers to help them set up a bingo group. While the tenants, presumably, wanted better housing, it looked as if they were not motivated to take collective action to do anything about it, at least at that time. The workers had allowed their own judgements about what could most benefit the estate to prevent them perceiving that the tenants were not where they, the community workers, 'were at'.

This is the central paradox of community work. On the one hand, effective community development work can only take place if the members of the community take prime responsibility for the action. On the other hand, what the members of the community want to do is often different from what the community workers think they should do!

Community workers who think the community has a particular need but find that, at a particular time, the community will not work to achieve it have a simple, if painful, choice. On the one hand they can seek to achieve it themselves by taking an organising or social planning role. On the other hand they can wait and 'sow seeds' until some people in the community are ready to 'own' what the worker thinks they should own. A worker in such a situation might also work with the community on priorities it identified but which were not his or hers.

Conclusion

This paradox is complicated in practice because, as community workers, we are often so enthusiastic about our own objectives for the community that we fail to perceive that the community members do not share that enthusiasm or that they will attend meetings only if somebody else (for example, the community worker) leads. This mistake is easy to make, partly because community members will often tell a worker what they think he or she wants to hear.

What is community work for?

Community work can perhaps best be described, first, as a set of values and, secondly, as a set of techniques, skills and approaches which are linked to those values. The values are to do with justice, respect, democracy, love, empowering and 'getting a better deal' for people who in some way are disadvantaged. The techniques are primarily to do with establishing relationships with such people (and others), understanding how they see the world and finding ways *to assist them to help themselves* which need not exclude, some of the time, doing things 'for' them.

The values of some community workers seem to be primarily political. In Britain, for instance, particularly in the 1970s and 1980s, many community workers seemed to be motivated to do their work from a socialist or feminist analysis of society. Other workers come at the practice of community work from a different kind of value system or ideology, pacifism or Christianity, for example (see, for instance, Kelly, 1993 and Kelly and Sewell, 1996). Yet others seem to come at community work from what might be called simpler values, a concern to do a bit of good in the world, for instance, or a concern to make the existing system work better for the poor. (See Alinsky's writings, 1969 and 1972 for an example of this last perspective.)

In reality, community work appeals to people with a variety of different ideologies. However, there is only a loose connection between an ideology and a particular approach to practice. In any real-life situation there will be many pressures and constraints on a worker to operate in some ways rather than others. Whatever their ideology, effective practitioners need to select those actions which seem most likely to help the members of a particular community get a better deal for themselves and become more confident and skilled, and which also change or improve local government or other systems to the benefit of that community. While the values of community workers will quite legitimately influence their priorities, they also have to be very pragmatic about choosing which approach is likely to work best.

Whether because of ideology, personal attributes or personality type, some community workers are very effective at, and predisposed towards, building relationships with members of communities at local level and staying in the background. Others may be good trainers. Others are good at 'making things happen'. Others are good at helping marginalised groups fight for their rights. Yet others are good at 'working the system' to benefit the community. To a degree, therefore, it makes sense for workers to work to their strengths, as long as that is appropriate to the local situation.

Whatever their values, predispositions and existing skills, community workers must also be 'Jacks of all trades' who are prepared to learn new approaches and bring them into play in different circumstances.

The theory (such as it is) and practice of community work have their roots in many different places: adult education, the British colonies, Liberation Theology, mid-20th century Western European Marxism, social work, civil rights, pacifism, British philanthropic movements (such as settlements), feminism, and probably others. Within the wide range of philosophies or ideologies (and the apparent absence of these) which underpin practice for particular workers, there is usually (and I believe there needs to be) a common concern about justice and the other values mentioned above. There is also a commonality between the various theoretical underpinnings of community work in that they are all based on helping people get a better deal, primarily by making this happen themselves, with all the problems, paradoxes and limitations there are on doing this in practice.

The problem of invisibility

It is relatively easy to observe an active community group by noting what it does. It is less easy to observe the painstaking work, often behind the scenes, which resulted in that group becoming effective. For this reason, among many others, it is difficult to demonstrate, to potential funders for instance, that community work makes a difference. There is, additionally, little good research which demonstrates a causal relationship between (paid) community work and effective (unpaid) community action and the link between these and, for example, better services.

In order to demonstrate the effectiveness of community work it is often necessary to make potential funders 'walk the streets' with you. That is, you have to take them to see effective projects and schemes and then carefully talk through with them the reasons why the particular scheme was successful. Community workers need to develop the skills of making community work processes more visible.

Start-stop ... start

Many of the community work projects which do exist are often short-term: three years at most. It will be six months, at least, before the project is 'up and running'. It will be at least another six months before much of value is delivered, probably longer. And after another year and a half the staff will be looking around for new jobs. Much of any good which has been done may well be unsustainable, as a result of which the community-run initiatives supported by the staff run down, leaving a very disillusioned community. Then, three years later, a similar initiative starts in the same area and repeats the process!

Arguably, such projects cause more harm than good. There is, additionally, a limit to what one, probably underpaid and poorly resourced, worker can achieve. Some individuals are excellent at their jobs. But they eventually leave. Others are not so excellent. Others may be ineffective for longish periods through illness or domestic problems.

For these reasons, community work needs to become strategic, long-term and integral to the organisations which seek to deliver it. In Britain, there is still only limited understanding of the above points, leading sometimes to relatively ineffective programmes. While community work practitioners need to learn to be as effective as possible, its sponsors need to learn to structure it in such a way that it makes a lasting difference.

2

Designing the Intervention and Finding Out What People Want

Designing the intervention

Project design often happens hurriedly, because funding bids may only be made to a particular source for a limited period of time, for instance. But this often creates problems for the future because the ideas of those most concerned to establish the initiative are unlikely to be shared by those whose continuing support is needed if the project is to be successful or to be continued after, say, three years. Because funding from external sources for special projects offers the opportunity of pulling more resources into an area, a major potential sponsor, a local authority, for example, may support a community work project without its officers and members understanding the implications. This almost inevitably results in unproductive conflict later on when the project outcomes turn out to be different from what those sponsors expected. It is important, therefore, when designing and seeking to obtain funding for a project or strategy to explain to the main power holders what the initiative is expected to achieve and the way it will run, in order to give a chance to all stakeholders to think about the implications.

There are a variety of techniques for determining the perceived needs and aspirations both of communities and of service providers, several of which are covered later in this chapter. On the one hand, some work of this kind should be carried out in the project design phase. On the other hand, this should be a continuous process too, and one which the staff take on, both when newly appointed and subsequently. Producing a 'pre-start' project plan in fine detail can be a waste of time and money, because workers on the ground will also need to gather their own information and because the opportunities and means of meeting community need can change quickly.

Depending on the nature of the initiative, it is also useful to seek to explain to the community what the initiative is for and to involve its members early on. However, if the community is not well organised, this may be difficult to do before the project starts because there are no staff to do this work and no organised group to explain it to. Also, if it is not certain that the project can go ahead, expectations can be raised and then later dashed. In such initiatives, the community consultation stage often has to come later, after the workers are appointed. We also need to remember that 'excluded' communities do not usually ask for community workers and do not generally understand how community work can help them until they have seen it working in practice. All these factors can make it difficult to involve the community in 'pre-start' project design.

It is important to commit the results of 'pre-start' research to paper, linking the rationale for the project with the methods of work, expected outcomes and how these will be monitored, drawing attention to any important implications or likely problems. Consideration should also be given, if possible, as to what will happen after the first, say, three years of the scheme.

This project design process can never be undertaken with too much care. A one-year preparation process should be an absolute minimum. In this process the main stakeholders should, ideally, develop a sense of ownership towards the initiative. If they do so, when more funding is required they will examine their own finances to see how far they can help. If, on the other hand, that sense of ownership is not developed, you will be going to them, cap in hand, three years later and will be competing with all the other schemes clamouring for their attention.

In order to win the support of major players you need to help them see how the initiative will help them meet *their* objectives for the community in question. In this process it can be useful to take them to see similar projects. Prepare such visits carefully, work out in advance what it is you want them to examine, brief your hosts accordingly and ensure that the visitors discuss and reflect on the experience afterwards.

You will probably also want these stakeholders on your management or advisory board to ensure that their sense of ownership continues.

Many people involved in community work are good at 'getting out there and doing the work' but less good at developing office procedures, setting up filing and recording systems, keeping appropriate accounts, ensuring there is adequate insurance for the office, mastering employment law, and so on. Suffice to say that giving attention to such issues early is time very well spent. If there is, say, a four-person project including secretary/administrator, it is often wise to employ the project leader first, followed, as soon as possible, by the secretary in order to ensure that such systems are in place, before engaging the other staff.

In a similar way, the project leader needs to learn about the principles of good staff management, supervision and team building, and to apply those when inducting the staff.

Contact-making – our bread and butter

However well a project has been prepared, the workers, once in post, have the task of deciding exactly what to do, even though their general focus will probably have been determined by their terms of reference. Also, because community workers control almost nothing, we need the support and goodwill of as many other people as possible if we want to get anything done. Unless we take care to cultivate this goodwill and mutual understanding widely, and to develop a sense of ownership in others about what we want to achieve, we may find that the natural conservatism and resistance to change of most people will turn into opposition. Therefore, it is necessary, initially at least, to establish contacts with people of like mind. We cannot know who has the time, inclination, resources and connections needed to undertake a successful piece of work unless we are systematically making and remaking contacts at all levels.

Community work could also be described as permanent innovation. We need to be on the lookout, not only for people with whom an alliance can be built, but also for new ideas, which tends to occur when we are continually extending our contacts with a wide range of people.

One day a probation officer dropped in to see me at our neighbourhood centre. We arranged a more formal meeting with his team during which they expressed concern that probationers in the locality had to travel a long way to report to the probation office. After further discussion we arranged to make our centre available once a week for the probation department to use as a reporting centre.

But is not contact-making just common sense? Perhaps it is, but common sense is not that common! Also, the pressures on professional staff today, which are often to do with achieving particular targets, can make it difficult for us to find the time to carry out permanent contact-making without a fixed agenda.

By trial and error I found that the most important principles or rules to follow (whether with professionals or community members) are:

Rule 1: Never pass up the opportunity to make or renew a contact – unless you are fairly sure that to do so will damage another area of work. Also, it is not usually a good idea to ask a new contact for something you want at the first meeting. Concentrate more on finding out how they see the situation and where their self-interest is. You may later be able to fit what you want to do into their self-interest.

Rule 2: Consider first and foremost what impression you are making. How we dress, for instance, is a statement about ourselves, and people make assumptions about us from it. Consider whether you are having the desired effect on the other person.

Punctuality is vital. People in authority may write us off before we start if we turn up half an hour late for the first meeting. Equally, people will not take us seriously if we agree to do something and fail to do it. Say well in advance if you are not able to honour a commitment. We need to be regarded as being credible by as many people as possible.

Rule 3: Learn how to listen and observe. By 'listening' I am referring not only to the process of taking in the explicit content of what someone is saying but also to understanding what may only be implied. Is the person just saying what they think you want to hear? What are they conveying about their relationships with other residents or their family or, in the case of a local government official, other departments? Most important of all, for initial contacts with community members, what are they conveying about both their motivation and their ability to take organisational responsibility?

When we are listening to another person talk we do not only use our ears, we speak too, and it may often be necessary to steer the other person round to discuss matters we want to discuss. Good listening is the art, first, of registering the explicit and implicit content of what a person is saying and, secondly, assessing or interpreting it, perhaps tentatively at first. Good listening does not mean we do not contribute. Neither does it mean we cannot at least partly structure what is being said.

Listening to ourselves is equally important. We cannot perceive others accurately unless we are in touch with our own feelings. Do we find this person boring? Do we find we become angry when he or she is talking? Do we feel threatened? It is also important to try to understand what the other person is feeling, to put ourselves in their place. Whatever we want from the meeting – information, a relationship, money – we are more likely to get it if we can empathise in this way.

We have to train ourselves to notice not only how we affect other people, but also how they in turn react to other parties. At an important meeting I once held with a county councillor, the assistant county clerk looked bored. That indicated something about the relationship between the councillor and that officer, a point useful for me to remember at a later date perhaps.

Notice where people sit, how they arrange their offices and rooms, what newspaper they read, what pictures they have on the wall, and so on. For many of us this means practice; it does not come naturally. Neighbourhood community workers also need to notice what is going on in the locality. If people appear with theodolites, ask them what they are doing – it may be the first sign that a new road scheme is being considered. It can be useful to know what shops are closing, what houses are vacant and so on: in short, indications of the changes that are continually taking place in a locality. It is also important to check the local paper for applications for planning permission, and other proposals for the area.

You need a systematic information gathering system too. I read the main newspaper of Wales daily because my job is to promote community work in Wales. Similarly a community worker operating in a community with a massive drugs problem would need to learn about that scene, or, if they were operating in Northern Ireland at the time of the troubles, how the paramilitary organisations operated.

We also need to guard against becoming too parochial. Workers doing similar jobs in other parts of the country will have discovered many ways of dealing with situations which you are meeting for the first time. So, find ways of learning from them.

Rule 4: Create opportunities for establishing personal contacts. For neighbourhood workers the rule could be rephrased: *Walk, don't ride.* If you wish to make contacts in a structured way and to notice changes, it is good practice to walk around the area regularly. There are, of course, times when it is more appropriate to walk than others, in summer for instance, and it is important to plan contact-making accordingly. If you are not working at neighbourhood level you need to put yourself in situations where you have time to meet people informally but in a systematic way.

Rule 5: In order to get we must give. Initial meetings can sometimes be problematic, and they need to be thought about carefully in advance. For instance, a local councillor may feel that the worker is a threat. Local residents may feel uncomfortable if workers seem vague about what their purpose is. Think about how you can best put yourself across, and reflect afterwards whether it worked.

On the one hand, it is best to be as natural as possible when meeting people for the first time so that a relationship is established. On the other hand, in many such meetings, our purpose is to get something from the other person, even if only information. But people give best if they get something in return. It may be useful to encourage them to talk first about what interests them: their work, their hobbies, their family, perhaps. For many men, and some women, football is a great ice-breaker, for instance. It can also be a good idea to learn about the interests of the person you are meeting beforehand so that you can have a good chance of creating some rapport quickly by mentioning certain topics.

Most importantly, however, we need to be genuinely interested in the people we are meeting.

I contacted a local headteacher shortly after he took up his post, explained my role and made tactful suggestions that he and his staff might get more involved in the community. Nothing doing! Much later he complained to me that parents would not visit the school on open evenings. I listened patiently and eventually asked whether he thought they would come to our neighbourhood centre if a teacher was available there. He became interested and eventually an agreement was made to use our centre. Only when I could help him was he prepared to listen to me.

Rule 6: Do not believe everything people say. A member of a community group would sometimes tell me privately that they were going to resign soon, but never actually did so. While they were talking to me it might have been their full intention to resign because they were particularly aware at that moment of the frustrations of being a group member. But at other times they would have looked at their membership of the group in different ways and become more aware of the disadvantages of leaving: so when it came to the crunch they would not resign. Store information like this until it is corroborated by information from other sources or until intentions do indeed become action. Some people will also lie in order to save face when under pressure, or will assert the opposite of what is actually the case because they want to convince us that they 'always consult widely', for instance.

A community profile

Purpose

The purpose of a community profile is, first, to gather *information* about the needs of a locality and, second, to provide the basis for an *analysis* of possible courses of action. However, in the process of gathering the relevant information, we make contact with many people, and some of those contacts are likely to be the starting-point for action. We may discover that several local people are concerned about the lack of play-space and are prepared to do something about it, for example. The community-profile stage may then overlap with the action stage.

We may be under external and internal pressure to get on quickly with the job and, therefore, to omit or skimp on the community profile. This is particularly dangerous when we succeed another community worker. When I started out as a neighbourhood worker, I worked largely from the basis of contacts left by my predecessor and never stood back, reviewed my overall strategy or developed my own contacts. I made many mistakes as a result, such as setting up a tenants' association which nobody wanted!

Two types of information are required for a community profile, hard and soft. Hard information consists of quantified data and can be obtained from official reports such as the census. Soft information is more subjective and consists largely of opinions. On the one hand, it is no good obtaining detailed housing statistics relating to the locality unless we know the views of residents about their housing needs. On the other hand, it would not be the wisest course of action to try to set up an organisation for one-parent families without making an attempt to ascertain the approximate number of such families in the first place.

Some community profiles (or community-needs analyses – there are several different names) relate to small neighbourhoods, others to whole counties. Others may relate to a community of interest or need. Nevertheless, whatever the context, the principles covered here can be adapted to most situations.

Gathering information in the worker's own agency

While a community worker will normally have a specific job description, different colleagues may, in reality, have differing expectations of him or her. Also, the job description may be unrealistic. So it is useful to start by discovering the views of one's colleagues. At the same time as establishing relationships with colleagues it is necessary to read any relevant agency records. Very soon, however, a problem crops up. The information may not be compiled in such a way as to break down as easily as is required. For instance, unemployment figures may cover a different area from the neighbourhood with which the project is concerned. We then have to decide whether the data are so important that we are prepared to spend time going back to the original sources, which may not be easy to do.

It is also important to look at past reports and planning documents for the area. If we know how the area has been perceived over time we should be able to predict more accurately how our own agency and others will react to our proposed work. We should also know whether a certain approach was once tried and had failed.

Planning sections of local authorities will often make relevant reports available, together with other statistical data. It is useful to contact such officials personally. They are usually pleased to help.

It is also necessary to obtain from colleagues in the agency their perception of needs in the area, information about who holds power, who to go through to get things done, who is sympathetic to your approach, who to get on your side and so on. Talk to a range of people from different levels and particularly to people who may be sceptical about community work. At the same time, it is necessary to ask people if they can suggest further contacts in other organisations or in the target community. By this process we establish our own network of contacts. However, we also need to be clear *why* we are going to see someone. An interview is frustrating for both sides if neither party knows why it is taking place. You also need to work out when to stop gathering information because it can become a never-ending process. The same process needs to be carried out with other relevant agencies.

Gathering hard information

It is normally useful to know the size and age structure of the population and other demographic data. Some of this information will be in the census which should be in the public library. It is useful, also, to be able to work out trends, whether the black population, for example, is increasing, which may mean referring to previous censuses as well. It could also help to know, for instance, how the figures for sickness or infant mortality compare with the area as a whole and with the country as a whole. But we should use our own initiative too. School rolls may provide information about the child population, and it might be possible to find a head teacher who can provide information that reveals year-to-year changes which the census does not. It can also be useful to know the socio-economic class structure and unemployment rates for men, women and school leavers.

Another reason for gathering this 'hard' information is because you may need it later for a funding application.

An understanding of the local economic structure is basic in analysing the needs and problems of a community. It can be useful to know where people tend to work, what kind of pay they get whether local employers are contracting or expanding and so on. This helps to develop a general feeling about the industrial scene. The local authority economic development department ought to be able to help here.

It can be useful to find out the age of the housing, the degree to which houses contain basic facilities, the degree of overcrowding and patterns of multi-occupation and whether the housing is 'social', privately rented or owner-occupied. Information about the local authority's housing policies may also be useful – their allocation and transfer policies, for example. Local authority housing-department staff, committee minutes and the annual reports of the housing manager to the council may provide this information.

Find out which councillors represent the neighbourhood and who the 'heavyweight' councillors are. How strong are the various political parties on the council? Much of this information can be obtained from the town hall information office and the rest from speaking with friendly politicians, officials or activists who have been around for a long time. It could be useful to observe a council meeting or read past council minutes.

Information also needs to be obtained about all statutory agencies which are located in or which serve the area: health centres, police, youth centres and public transport, for example. Whenever possible, go and talk to the relevant personnel in these agencies.

Non-statutory organisations are so many and varied that they are difficult to categorise. There are voluntary organisations employing professionals, such as the National Society for the Prevention of Cruelty to Children. There are commercial organisations, such as working men's clubs, and commercially run opportunities for leisure-time pursuits, such as bingo halls. There are also faith groups and political organisations. Finally there is a plethora of community and voluntary organisations – tenants' associations and playgroups, for example – and more traditional organisations, such as the Women's Royal Voluntary Service, and organisations for disabled people which may be part of a national structure. This information can be discovered mainly by asking around and exploring the area. The public library may also be able to help. Buy a street map too.

To find out what it is like to be a resident in a particular locality, it is often quite a good idea to travel around a bit by bus or approach estate agents about accommodation. Try to get a feel of what it is like to be a local resident.

In obtaining this information we meet a wide range of people, and we need to take advantage of these contacts to build up our stock of soft information. What do they think are the needs of the area? What is their position in their organisation? What are the pet schemes they want to back? What are they touchy about? What was tried in the past and what was the result? We should also be recording the information we obtain conscientiously, because the next stage is to try to marry it all together into an analysis which will lead to action.

Gathering information from residents

Our contacts with other professionals may provide us with the names of several people who are or were active in the community, and it is important to follow them up. To introduce ourselves we can usually mention the person who referred us to them. Nevertheless we have to think about how we describe ourselves. It is accurate but often inappropriate at an initial meeting to say that we have come to help them join with other residents in taking action on issues they are concerned about. But over time we need to find ways of conveying this, perhaps by giving examples of concrete ways in which we could help. One way is to engage them in general conversation and gradually slip in the points we want to make. At this stage, however, we are mainly wanting general information; we want to pick their brains about the history of community action in the area, what factions there are and what is currently going on; we want to know if they can put us in touch with other people who can give us more information. This process of building up contacts one from the other is sometimes called 'snowballing' or 'chain referral'.

While we may wish to encourage some of our contacts to become involved in community action, attempting to 'push' people into community action before they are ready may frighten them off. At this stage we are students; we are learning.

Many people are quite pleased to talk about themselves, and the problem is often stopping them! Another problem may be to keep them on the subject of community needs rather than their other interests. On the other hand we have to allow people to talk about what *they* want in order to establish a relationship. If you consider that public transport is inadequate, you might introduce the subject by asking whether it is easy to get into town and back. That way you are guiding the discussion but not imposing a rigid structure. An opportunity may also occur for workers to demonstrate their commitment. If, for example, the contact says there used to be a playgroup run by Mrs. X but since it closed the equipment seems to have got lost, the worker could offer to visit Mrs. X to try to discover the whereabouts of the equipment. Actions like this are often more important than mere words in conveying what the worker is there for. At the same time you have to take care that you do not spring too quickly into action, thus neglecting your strategic planning tasks and giving the impression that you are there to do things *for* people rather than to help them do things themselves.

The danger with 'snowballing' is that we may become familiar with only one network, since people will often put us in contact with their friends. Thus, it is important to make contacts in other ways too, by attending places where people naturally congregate – outside primary schools at the end of the school day, for instance. Other commonly used places are pubs or post offices, but there are many more possibilities. However, when making contacts by going to such places, one is also meeting with an unrepresentative group: women with young children, for example. Are the people one is meeting representative enough? Other factors affect this type of contact-making too. Some (usually female) community workers understandably feel unhappy chatting in public houses. On the other hand, some workers might be drawn to using public houses because of their liking of a pub atmosphere rather than because this was the best way of getting to know people. It is important to think about the methods we choose to make these contacts, as well as using our strengths.

Planned door-knocking is another method to consider. But it takes a great deal of time. If workers want open-ended discussions with as many residents as possible, they are likely to be in some houses for well over an hour. If they have to return later to houses where the occupant is initially out, it can take weeks to contact even half of the residents in a street. I once asked a student on placement to make contacts in this way in a street of 200 houses. It took about half of her three-month placement and resulted only in two major contacts.

One way to ease the first meeting with people when door-knocking is to put a leaflet through the door a day or so before you call (perhaps taking care to distinguish yourself from the council) stating who your are and what your business is. It is amazing how this can break the ice.

Contact-making does not necessarily produce quick or direct results. People participate when *they* are ready. The fact that a community worker has contacted them at a certain point may well provide them with more knowledge than they had before. You may have sown seeds which begin to germinate at a later date, perhaps next year when their children go to school and they have a little more time on their hands. It is also important not to make up our minds about people too quickly. A student on placement made an initially favourable contact with a vicar who promised a lot of help. On the other hand, a local councillor was very suspicious and was mentally 'written off' by the student. Later the vicar showed himself to be only interested in getting people into church whereas the councillor became helpful when she realised that the worker had a genuine commitment to the area. Many of the people with real power and commitment will not co-operate until you have shown yourself trustworthy and useful.

We really do have to discover what people themselves want before we can involve them effectively. They will not stay involved unless what they want to do coincides with what we want them to do. Unless we get this process right, we will have no one to work with, at any level!

Another way to discover the felt needs of residents is to use a survey, but this is very time-consuming. Above all, it is important to work out beforehand whether the survey is being used as a means of gathering 'soft' information more systematically, or whether the task is to produce a more objective measurement of need. Many community workers think they can do both at once, which is difficult. An objective survey must be carefully designed, especially if it is to cover intangible areas such as attitudes. It will need to be closed-ended, with questions like 'Do you mainly shop in this street/in this estate/in town/elsewhere?' The interviewer's task is to get clear answers to questions which can then be quantified. But if you are using the survey as a means of contacting residents and building up your store of soft information you will want to encourage respondents to talk at some length around the questions you ask. Thus, you will ask 'open-ended' questions such as 'What do you think of the shops in the area?' It is important to know which approach, or which combination of the two, is most appropriate to the task in hand. Sometimes an active residents' association can assist with this process and will carry out much of the work, as a result of which its members learn many useful skills. However, this requires a great deal of organisation and commitment from the community.

If you opt for a 'proper' survey to provide yourself with an accurate picture of need rather than the 'soft' variety, you should make sure you get an expert on social surveys to assist.

A further way to discover views about needs is to invite people to a small group discussion, ask them a series of questions and record their answers. Such 'focus' groups are increasingly used to produce information for community profiles.

An 'issue' profile

Henderson and Thomas (1987) discuss undertaking a 'broad angle' scan followed by a 'narrow angle' scan when discovering information. The broad angle scan provides general information. The narrow angle scan provides more detailed information relevant to the specific areas of work in which the worker expects to be involved. It is important to distinguish between the two because one can go on gathering information about a geographical area for ever, and it is necessary to undertake a community profile as economically as possible.

The principles for undertaking a community profile with a community of interest or need (for example, disabled people), which I prefer to call an issue profile in this context, are the same as for a geographical profile, namely:

- Gathering hard information.
- Gathering (soft) information from agencies dealing with that community.
- Gathering (mainly soft) information from *personal contact* with members of that community.

It takes little effort to sit down and work out how to do this systematically. A brainstorming exercise usually produces a good list of sources of information. In particular, there are national agencies such as: Women's Aid, the Commission for Racial Equality, Shelter, Mind, and so on, and contact with them can produce both hard data, including information on relevant laws, and also guidance about how to set up particular projects. More difficult to obtain, however, is statistical information for that community of need which relates to a particular county or city. However, relevant local authority departments are an obvious early port of call as are local support agencies, if they exist, which specialise in work with or for that group. (See Hawtin *et al.* (1994) for more on community profiling.)

Analysis, planning and organisation

A community profile is more than a collection of information. It is a
tool with which to build an analysis as a basis for action. The
information obtained has to be ordered, emphasising not only the
objective needs of the community but also the more subjective
perceptions of its members and others in order to identify opportunities for action. Unemployment may be an enormous problem, for
instance, but it may not be possible to help residents organise to do
something about it. If one or two residents expressed the desire for a
parent–teacher association (PTA), you would need to ask yourself
whether there would be much support from other residents or from
teachers; whether becoming involved with a PTA would fit in with
your priorities and those of your agency (and, if not, perhaps to refer
them elsewhere); whether the necessary resources were available,
and so on.

You should build up some alternative possibilities for action from
all the information you have gathered. Each alternative should
ideally contain an assessment of its own advantages and disadvantages. Then it should be possible to make a choice about which
alternatives to select. The factors influencing the decision about
what to get involved with are:

- your own assessment of needs (based on hard and soft data);
- what your agency expects;
- your own ideology, value system or skills (what you *want* and *feel*
  able to do);
- the likelihood of success and
- what at least some community members want to get done and
  seem motivated to work on.

Write down the advantages and disadvantages of each possible
action using these five headings in order to clarify which are the
most likely areas for productive action.

While community workers should write down their community
profile and discuss it with their manager before acting on it, community work can also proceed in a more opportunistic way. A
couple of local people seem interested in an idea and, with the
worker's help, call a meeting with friends to discuss it. In no time
at all a group gets off the ground. Community work happens like

that, and it always will. That can be excellent practice. But it can also be bad practice because, if workers are under external and internal pressure to get something done, they may be desperate to find an embryonic community group of any kind. You only realise later that the two residents who seemed keen to set up the group are fervently disliked by the rest of the community, or that you are spending all your working hours helping one group stay together while there are potentially more fruitful avenues to explore for which you no longer have the time.

Do-it-yourself community profiles?

There is a range of approaches where the community is assisted to undertake its own profile. JIGSO, operating in Wales, is a process where a worker brings together a group of people who are as representative as possible of the locality and helps them produce a questionnaire about community need. Local volunteers are then guided in a door-knocking and interviewing process, and the completed questionnaires are fed into a computer to produce a needs analysis. The task of the group which has been brought together around this process is then to act on the needs identified.

A similar process, 'Planning for Real', developed by the Neighbourhood Initiatives Foundation, is based primarily on the creation of a physical model of the community. Local people are then encouraged to move the parts of the model around saying what they want where. This can be a particularly useful, practical and motivating way of discovering how local people want their community physically improved. Walker (1998) describes similar processes where people are brought together in a public meeting, helped to create a mission statement and invited through a brainstorming process to identify community needs and then to prioritise the most feasible and desirable projects.

To a degree, such approaches are based on the premise that a community only needs a little help to get itself organised permanently. While most community action is autonomous, in many disadvantaged areas citizens need continuing help to build and maintain community-run organisations. For this reason, such approaches need to be seen as one tool among many in the community development process.

3

Working with Community Groups I: Helping People Set Up and Run Groups

Introduction

A community worker can do very little if community members are not motivated. If they are, you can do a great deal. However, getting something done usually requires the power and legitimacy of an organisation. Thus, community workers spend a good deal of their time helping community members set up and run organisations effectively.

Intensive work to set up a group

For me the most important stages in setting up an autonomous community group are:

1. contacting people and establishing an analysis of needs;
2. bringing people together, helping them identify specific needs and assisting them to develop the will to see that those needs are met;
3. helping them understand what will have to be done if those needs are to be met
4. helping them identify objectives;
5. helping them form and maintain an organisation suitable for meeting those objectives;
6. helping them identify and acquire resources (knowledge, skills, money, people, equipment);

7. helping them choose priorities, evaluate alternative lines of approach and design a plan of action, thus turning strategic objectives into a series of smaller objectives and tasks;

8. helping them divide these tasks between them and carry them out;

9. helping the members of the group feed back the results of their actions to the whole group which then has to evaluate those actions and adopt modified objectives.

While a generic worker can start with the open-ended brief suggested by this list, a specialised/sectoral worker may be bringing only certain types of people together, be working on specific issues, or have a very specific brief from the employing agency, to set up a drop-in centre for young people, for example. Thus, specialised/sectoral community workers may need to start further down the list and 'recruit' people to a specific project, rather than trying to discover what it is the community wants.

Bringing people together

Let us now assume that you, the worker, have carried out your needs analysis and have some idea of your own objectives. You may find that you spend months making contacts without finding an issue or activity on which community members seem prepared to take action. If that is the case, you will, at some point, have to consider whether there are any other ways to get a project going. On the other hand, you may find that a number of residents are concerned about the same problem. At this point you will need to work out whether you are prepared to help people organise to address it. If your answer is in the positive you will probably need to allocate about two days per week for the tasks outlined below.

It is not too difficult to get people talking at the level of general needs, but the task of getting them to think about doing something to alter the situation is more difficult. First of all it requires time. A worker who set up a successful women's group on an isolated housing estate spent many weeks visiting a large number of people individually (some, five times) before setting up the group.

When you are trying to discover if people have the motivation to become involved, you undertake a mixture of tasks. You try to identify points in the conversation when your contact expresses a concern about community problems, such as, the bus service. Then you may try to keep the conversation on this subject, probably by asking questions. 'What you said about the bus service – does anyone else feel the same?' 'Why do you think it is that the bus service is so poor?' 'Has anyone ever tried to do anything about it?' 'Have *you* ever thought of doing anything about it?' 'Would you be interested in meeting with a few others to see if anything could be done about it?' It might only be through a process of several meetings that a subject was covered in that detail, but during these early stages of contact-making your main objective will be to arouse the interest of people to take action. 'Hey, maybe there *is* something I could do after all' is the kind of feeling you want to evoke.

At this stage, if you are a generic community worker, you may be able to respond positively to a range of ideas that people suggest. However, as you and some of the individuals with whom you are in contact become motivated to take action on a particular issue, your objective changes somewhat. Now you are trying to see how far other people are interested in *that* issue. The next step is to bring such people together. Often two or three keen people will meet to discuss the idea further. This may well happen without your suggesting it and, if so, that is usually a good sign. They also need to understand it is *their* project, and you do not want to be seen as the leader. Let us say that you are in contact with three women who have expressed interest in doing something about children's play. One way of moving ahead is to try to get them to arrange the first meeting between themselves rather than doing it yourself, which also tests their commitment and ability. In practice, circumstances may dictate that you arrange the meeting, and many successful groups start that way, but this can be the slippery slope of worker over-involvement and the creation of dependence rather than autonomy in the people with whom you are working. On the other hand, some community members may have so little confidence they will not set up a group themselves. If you arrange the meeting and set up the group yourself you will need to move the group from dependence to autonomy later on – not always an easy task.

The people who are meeting together may already know each other, and that makes it easier for you in one way – but they may just chat. You need to encourage this informal interchange but you must also get them to focus on the needs which they are meeting to discuss. To do this you can throw in ideas, ask questions, make statements, tell them what you think they should be doing or provide information. It may take several meetings to get them to focus on needs and objectives, and they may find they are all interested in doing different things. Or, personality problems may emerge, making co-operation difficult. As a result, some of them may not come again. It is important, however, to keep up the momentum. Make sure that a date is arranged for the next meeting, before which you meet the members individually yet again and plan with some of them what the meeting is to achieve. Conversely, if you have decided that you do not wish to continue with this group, you can 'forget' to suggest a date for the next meeting!

With people who are strangers, each individual may initially feel uneasy in the company of the others, and you may have to break the ice. Ensuring that a cup of tea is offered can sometimes help. It also helps to think about what casual subjects of conversation they are likely to respond to. The art of conversing casually in this way comes with practice. If you are not naturally good at it, work at it! With a group of strangers there may be a 'testing out' period, and it might well take such a group longer to 'gel' than it would a group of people who already know each other.

Expanding the membership

Many groups start with two or three people and gradually build up to six or seven. When there are very few members everyone should try to recruit more members. The worker, especially, should try to bring in more people because existing members will tend to recruit friends, workmates and relations. Unless care is taken to recruit widely, community groups can become, or become seen as, cliques. Indeed, they often contain members of the same family.

Personal contact is the most important method of expanding the membership, but now there is something particular to 'sell', and you will want to recruit people with an interest in that issue. So at this stage, the worker, or the group, may try to get an article in the press or on local radio, or get posters put in shops. However, few people will come to a group where they know no one. Consequently, if you hear of people who might be interested, call to see them or try to get a member of the embryonic group to do so.

Focusing on one objective

Let us say there are enough people for the group to start firming up
on what it wants to do. A group tends to become a group and start
working out its objectives when it numbers five or six, and in many
ways this is the ideal size. However, members often become despond-
ent if they only get attendances of this number, and the worker
then has to find ways of convincing them that they are doing OK.
At this stage the desire to get something done is often unfocused,
which creates a dilemma. Should you allow the members to carry on
in that unfocused way and run the risk that those who are more
task-oriented will leave? Or should you try to get them to focus on
one issue and run the risk of pressurising them too soon? You will
learn this by getting it wrong a few times! However, it is useful for
workers to know their own predisposition so that they can guard
against it if necessary. Mine is to intervene too early. Therefore I
have to force myself to wait. Others have more of a laissez-faire
approach, which may also need modifying on occasion.

Some people who have never been involved in a group like this
before may lack confidence. The problem is to convince them they
have the ability to do anything at all and to boost their morale.
Also, people new to groups often want to achieve too much too
quickly. The group has agreed to focus on 'play', and one member
says in early July, 'Let's run a summer play scheme.' The rest agree
and decide with enthusiasm that it should start next Monday and
run daily for six weeks! The worker's role is to find a way of helping
groups adopt realistic objectives, such as, in this case, perhaps, a
one-week play scheme at the end of the holidays. Otherwise you
may have to do a great deal of organising yourself if the venture is to
be successful.

You now have to help the members turn their discontent into a
series of needs, the needs into objectives and the objectives into
tasks which are then allocated. You must also help them choose
between different priorities – to run a play scheme or press the
council to provide fixed play equipment, for example. The question
of resources also arises. How much money would be needed for a
play scheme and how would it be obtained? How many helpers
would be needed and who would recruit them? What are the time
and skill implications of this for the group members? Whose permission would be needed if the group wanted to use the school

playground and who will find out? A worker has to try to get the group to face questions like these, but it is their enthusiasm which keeps the group going at this point, and it is important not to extinguish that.

Nothing fails like failure

If possible the group must start with a success. To fail at the first attempt may result in the death of the group. The secretary of a community group once decided to hold a sponsored walk. I knew he was organising it badly and tried several times to encourage him to make better preparations. But he did not want to listen. It was an absolute disaster. Only a few walkers turned up and no one paid the money they collected to the group. Sometimes that is the only way to learn. But that community leader never ran another sponsored walk!

Directive democracy?

In some cases the natural process of community group formation involves one or two group members (not the community worker) doing most of the organisational work, failing to ensure that new members are recruited and generally doing a poor job. Some community groups also fail to achieve their stated objectives.

The classic role of the community development worker is, in a 'non-directive' fashion, to suggest ways in which the group can be a bit more effective. This process certainly works, but only to a degree, and there is a case for a worker, in certain situations, to take a role which is more directive. Groups which are effective are difficult to create. Professional community workers should make sure they understand the processes and the types of organisational arrangements necessary for achieving effective democratic collective action in relation to the issues with which they are concerned. In situations where it is vital for a particular structure to be adopted and for the group members to have certain capabilities, the worker may need to agree a contract with the group to help them structure themselves, to *train* them perhaps in how to organise themselves, and not to work with them on any other basis. Thus the worker becomes a kind of organisational consultant or trainer, though the teaching style would need to be appropriate to the situation, to allow for discussion and so on.

A funder agreed to provide £3,000 to a community organisation for a study into the feasibility of establishing a business, on the basis that its members agreed to undertake some of the feasibility work themselves. They also had to agree to restructure their organisation with a consultant's help so as to be more geared to running business activities. The money was released in three tranches of £1,000 in stages as the agreed tasks were completed.

As community organisations aim, for instance, to establish credit unions, manage housing, tender for contracts or run regeneration programmes, this type of approach may become more and more necessary.

Community groups are sometimes run in an authoritarian manner by one or two leaders. They may discriminate against certain individuals or other groups and only pursue the narrow self-interest of a few of their members in their relations with public agencies or other communities. Unfortunately, once a group of this type emerges, it is difficult to change. There is a case, therefore, for a worker, in certain situations at least, to take a directive line from the start, to ensure that the group members understand and are committed to democratic values and are prepared to operate in ways which are respectful of, in particular, other community members. This approach requires the worker to take a somewhat didactic role, in a sense as a 'trainer' in democratic practice. However, such an approach is not often taken in the UK, perhaps partly because it is often so difficult to find community members willing to take leadership roles that workers tend to encourage whoever seems willing, even if they are not suitable. Also, because the worker may have to work hard to earn the trust of potential community leaders, it is very difficult to appear to be criticising them.

Community workers who are serious about encouraging local democratic practice might consider adopting a more directive approach to creating appropriate structures and processes, because these tend not to occur naturally. However, this approach requires the worker to agree with the group that this is to be his or her role. I also suggest that people new to community work should only try this if they have good supervision. (See Chapter 7 for more on these points.)

Organisational and interactional skills

If a community group decided to ask the local authority to provide a playground, the worker should immediately begin to think of the practicalities. Where could it be sited? Would it be vandalised? Would the council listen to a group of only six or is a public meeting or some other form of legitimation needed? What other support and evidence of need would be necessary to convince the authorities? What kind of opposition should be expected? What kind of organisation is needed to carry out this job? Do we need one person to write letters? Do we need to keep a record of decisions? Do we need a treasurer at this stage? Is headed notepaper necessary? The group members will think of some of these points but there are likely to be gaps in their thinking. For instance, they may decide that a particular action will be taken but omit to decide who will do it, as a result of which it is not done. Our job is to advise on these organisational questions.

As community workers we also need the ability to form relationships with other people in such a way that they will listen to and take action on our advice. We use these interactional skills together with our organisational skills to help the group do its own analysis, planning and organisation. If we wish to communicate with other people we must be able to empathise with them while retaining a degree of detachment. We must not be so full of what we want to say that we do not see Fred and Joe exchanging angry looks or notice that Joan has been very quiet that evening. We need also to be aware of the background of the people with whom we are working because that helps us to understand their thoughts and feelings. Then we are more likely to make appropriate rather than inappropriate comments.

Another important skill is saying clearly, simply and briefly what we mean. A common failing is using abbreviations unfamiliar to the audience. A related skill is learning to talk in parables and to use concrete rather than abstract words. We need to become aware of the words we use and to work on these communication skills. Consider videoing a community group meeting to help you with this, for instance (with permission, of course).

The worker's role in meetings

During group meetings a community worker's job is to help the group move smoothly through the business. You may well have met

with some members beforehand to plan the meeting, and they may
be looking to you for support. You will be aware that new members,
or other members who are not within the inner circle, have less
knowledge than those who have prepared the meeting, and you will
want to make sure that they also understand and contribute to the
proceedings. Think also about what *you* want to achieve. But your
plan must be open to alteration in the light of changing circumstances. If you anticipate a difficult meeting try to predict what the
difficulties will be and work out how to deal with them.

One important aspect of being a facilitator is asking questions,
such as, 'How many people would we need on the gate for the
carnival?' or 'Do we need to get permission to mount a demonstration outside the town hall?' The process of questioning can help
people clarify their own thoughts, which forms a necessary basis for
action. However, it does not always result in the group seeing the
point, and a more involved role is often required, when the worker
appears to be behaving more like one of the group, by making
suggestions or arguing the case for a particular approach. There
may also be times when you are sure the group is about to make a
mistake about which you want to warn the members firmly.

When using this 'facilitative' approach you are helping the group
members do things *their* way. However, you should not conceal
your own views. If you do, you may be perceived as vague and
ineffectual. Rather, state your view briefly, and only once if possible, while indicating that it is up to the group to make its own
decisions.

It is also necessary to allow group members to work things out at
their own pace. They may sometimes take half an hour to reach a
decision you could have taken in three minutes. That is one way in
which people learn.

Make clear the role you see yourself playing. If you have
explained that your objective is to work only for a short time helping a group get off the ground and then to withdraw, its members
have at least some chance of accepting, rejecting or negotiating
about what is offered, and there is less danger of conflicts arising
from differing expectations.

People new to groups tend not to think and act as part of the
group when they are outside it. During the early meetings of an Age
Concern group, Marion used to say, 'I've run a bingo session in my
house. Here's two pounds.' Although not previously sanctioned by

the group, Marion's actions did no harm. But other independent actions can be disastrous. One of our tasks is to teach group members how to liaise with each other between meetings, to sound out ideas with each other, to plan together and to divide tasks among them.

Work with individual group members

You will often need to spend time with a group's key members, helping them to work out agendas, implement decisions taken by the last meeting and so on. Very often a member agrees in a meeting to perform a task which they have not fully thought through and which may even be impossible. They may then not do it and give a lame excuse at the next meeting. For instance, a member might have agreed to write to the housing manager on a particular issue. However, the worker knows that this member is not accustomed to writing letters of that nature and so decides to offer help.

People new to groups often talk a great deal about what they plan to do but do not get around to carrying it out. Eric was 'all talk' for some months and I had given up hope that he would ever act. Then suddenly he started doing things; it was as if the talk was a preparation for the action. (But some talkers never 'do'.)

Some community group leaders put on a brave face and speak with assurance even when they are unsure. Such people can be difficult to work with because they feel too threatened to admit they need assistance. I often found myself almost colluding with such group members when they blamed other people for problems in the group for which they themselves were responsible. Any attempt by me to try to point out where their own actions had created the problem was so often met with a denial that I gave up trying to influence them directly and found other ways. When I wanted to influence one such community leader, I used to say (privately) to his wife something like: 'I've been wondering whether the group should try such and such. What would Ted think of this?' Sometimes Ted would approach me a month later and say 'Alan, I've had this great idea...'

Other group members rely too much on the worker and are reluctant to take responsibility themselves. To take the example of writing a letter to the housing manager, some people will always manage to get the worker to do it. In such a case, ways must be found of getting them to do it themselves, such as, by saying 'This time I'll do it, if you like. But let's work on it together so that next time you can do it yourself'. If you have initially spelt out that your role is to help the group become independent your task should be relatively easy.

Authoritarian community group leaders are often tolerated because of the amount of work they do. But sometimes they go too far and the other members take them to task. At this stage, this kind of leader often becomes angry and threatens to resign. Such people also sometimes feel threatened when new people join the group, particularly people with ability and, in effect, try to exclude them. They may also be suspicious of a community worker and perceive him or her as a threat. If you have any choice in the matter, think carefully whether a particular local person is somebody through whom and with whom you want to work before you encourage him or her to take a leadership role. It is not easy to change a difficult situation later on.

Dividing up or delegating tasks is difficult for most groups. Delegation requires thought about which tasks would be suitable, bearing in mind the abilities of the person who is to carry them out. If that person is not experienced, their skills and confidence have to be built up slowly, which requires time, effort and some skill. This partly explains why the leaders of community groups often fail to 'train' future leaders.

Structuring the group

You may need to give considerable attention to assisting existing and potential leaders to work together and encouraging appropriate delegation.

On the one hand, people who are unused to committees should not be rushed into formal procedures. On the other hand, if, for instance, a group is handling large amounts of money, representing the views of the community on a regeneration forum or mounting a campaign which needs careful co-ordination and planning, a clear delineation of roles and division of responsibility along the lines of a formal committee is necessary.

The device of a committee was invented to help a group of people take decisions in the most effective and democratic way. That is why formal organisations have constitutions and officers and why they adopt procedures such as minutes, agendas, and so on. Whatever structure a group adopts, it must be designed to take the kinds of decisions and actions which that group needs to take.

If you are concerned that some members may be afraid of a formal committee structure but think that something is needed to stop meetings degenerating into unstructured chat sessions, you should discuss the matter with the members. You might suggest they make a list of the items for discussion at the beginning of the meeting and that someone keeps a record of decisions. Only later might you say that those were an agenda and minutes.

Some workers believe it is important to rotate roles frequently in groups. However, I have rarely seen this work well, which is due, I think, to the tension between participation and effectiveness. There may be one person in a group who is quite good at chairing meetings. Thus, the meeting may be best chaired if he or she does it for, say, a year. The problem is even bigger with the roles of secretary and treasurer where continuity is particularly important.

Some community workers advocate non-hierarchical or 'collective organisation' as opposed to bureaucratic, hierarchical or 'top down' organisation. In some situations, non-hierarchical organisations can work but they are often problematic, particularly when there are disagreements between members or one is underperforming. Such problems can take many hours to resolve. Workers contemplating establishing this kind of organisation should discuss the approach they intend to take with others who have worked in collectives before they go ahead. (See Edwards, 1984, and Landry *et al.*, 1985, for some of the pitfalls involved in establishing non-hierarchical forms of organisation, but also Stanton, 1989, for a thorough and positive account of collective working.)

Strictly non-hierarchical groups tend not to be effective at achieving complex instrumental tasks. On the other hand, all groups and organisations have to allow for consultation and influence both laterally and vertically. Also, on a much larger scale, organisations such as local authorities are increasingly seeking to find consultative and co-operative ways of operating and of relating these to traditional line management. A great deal of work still needs to be done to find ways in which organisations of all kinds can be democratic, effective and humane.

In any group of ten people or more an 'inner core' tends to dominate, and the rest feel excluded. It is important to consider ways in which all members can be involved, so that they feel part of the group and are less likely to drop out. On the other hand, one person, as a minimum, has to ensure that the group's tasks are completed.

Any enterprise needs leadership, participation and expertise if it is to be effective, whether that is a community group or a local authority. These three are all in tension, however, and if any one of them is too dominant the whole enterprise suffers. Community workers need to be aware of the need to keep all three in balance.

The need for hard resources and technical assistance

Community groups often need: equipment, photocopying facilities, a room to meet, information (about housing legislation, for instance), help from professionals such as lawyers, and many other practical resources. Many things which seem small in themselves, such as the use of a telephone or word processor, are vital for community groups, and workers need, if possible, to provide access to these. When a group is starting off it may also need money, to book a room, for example, and it is very useful if community workers have 'pump-priming' funds which they can make available for such purposes. The provision of hard resources also helps convince people that the worker really is on their side.

In Britain there now exist several agencies, such as, the Community Design Service and the Professional Firms Group of Business in the Community, which give 'technical assistance' to community groups. It is worth finding out about what exists in your area and how it can be tapped. The local council for voluntary service or the community development department of the local authority (if it exists) may be able to help.

There are now also many helpful booklets covering a myriad of practical issues which community groups face. It is important for a worker to contact national support agencies such as, in Britain, the Standing Conference for Community Development, the Community Development Foundation, Community Matters, the National Council for Voluntary Organisations and others, which can, usually quite quickly, indicate what exists and how to get hold of it. A word of caution, however. Some community group members may need help to work through a booklet or to select appropriately from it. The fact that something is written down does not necessarily mean that people understand what it says. Ways have to be found of helping people 'own' something, usually by relating it to a practical situation within their experience.

To summarise the three preceding sections, workers who are helping a new group get off the ground will:

1. attend (at least some) group meetings and help the group adopt an appropriate structure, become clear about what it wants to do and take decisions;
2. work with the members, mainly the leaders, by building their confidence, helping them plan meetings and carry out what the group has decided;
3. perform a number of tasks *for* the group, such as, discovering information or making contacts.

In addition, you may be recruiting new members and promoting the interests of the group more generally.

Creating a constituency – public meetings, personal contact and newsletters

When a group proposes to act on behalf of the community, its members often consider it necessary to ensure community support by holding a public meeting, of which a major purpose may be to elect a committee. In practice, however, public meetings can be problematic. It is sometimes possible to hold a successful public meeting with limited preparation. But inadequate preparation can often result in: a poor turnout and despondency among the group members, an unruly meeting, which the organisers cannot control or a meeting monopolised by one or two dominant individuals, which fails to achieve its objectives. There are also a number of other factors which cannot be controlled – the weather, and popular TV programmes, for example.

A public meeting must be well publicised, by putting notices through doors and in shop windows, through announcements on local radio, by loudspeaker van perhaps, and most important, by word of mouth. You need to use your imagination here. Sometimes schools will give children notices to take home, for instance.

Making arrangements, like booking a room, can sometimes be very time-consuming and cause problems, such as, when you find the only room available is a primary school classroom with tiny chairs or that you cannot use the tea-making facilities. Considerations like the layout of the chairs are important. Most likely you will not want serried ranks of chairs but a semi-circle. That means someone must be on hand early to organise things.

The most important question is how to balance the democracy of a public meeting with control by the organising group. If possible, one of the members of the existing group should chair the meeting. But they will probably be reluctant to do this if they have not done so before. Also they might not be a very effective chair. If an inexperienced community member is going to chair the meeting, the worker may need to spend time helping them prepare for various eventualities – how to cope with dominant councillors, for example. Community workers also need to think about the most appropriate role to take themselves in such situations.

Electing a committee at a public meeting can be problematic. It is imperative for the embryonic group to have some names in advance to put forward, especially for officers, because sometimes totally unsuitable people are nominated or there are no nominations. At the same time, the process should be seen to be democratic.

If a meeting is seen as rigged, support may vanish. Before one important meeting (not a public meeting) I had prepared with a keen group member 'our' nominations for secretary, treasurer and chair. Instead of asking for nominations for each office, as a result of which everyone could have made suggestions and during which either of us could have suggested 'our' nominations, he took out the piece of paper on which I had written our nominations and said, to my considerable embarrassment, that these were the people he and I thought should take the offices! I had failed to prepare this person adequately because I had *assumed* he would know how to handle the situation.

When choosing officers for a group it is usually best to discuss and agree the process by which they will be selected or elected rather than merely asking for nominations. If this is not done someone is likely to say, 'Tom, why don't you become the chair?' Tom probably feels constrained to say 'yes' while others feel constrained to agree, even though Tom may not be the most appropriate person.

Community groups often become out-of-touch cliques, and so it is important to help them retain their constituency. The best way is if the members have continuing personal contact with the rest of the community. It is often necessary too, to have annual meetings where a new committee can be elected and where the actions of the group are open to scrutiny, but such meetings are often not well attended. Another way is for the group to arrange representation according to streets. However, it is rare for each street representative to report back to their constituency of neighbours. Other groups collect regular subscriptions or raise money through a door-to-door lottery. Public events, such as exhibitions, jumble sales or summer fêtes also publicise the group and arouse interest in the community. However, all of this takes lots of time and good quality organisation.

Shortly after I started work as a fieldworker I asked residents whether a local newsletter would be a good idea. They thought it was but did not say they would run it. I had the choice either to wait until they were ready or to run it myself. I chose the latter but made sure they contributed articles. Although many community workers claim that local people run the newsletter, it is often the community workers who do this. A newsletter may well be of high enough priority for a worker to do it if local people cannot. But I found that producing one copy took about a week's work spread over two months. It also takes time for a newsletter to become well known, so magic results should not be expected. It should be kept simple and come out at regular, though not necessarily frequent intervals. (See Armstrong *et al.*, 1976, and Lowndes, 1982, for more on newsletters.)

Relationships with the outside world

Community workers ought to have knowledge of the workings of large organisations and know, for example, that particular policies and procedures are laid down which cannot easily be bypassed, at least by community groups. Letters stay at the bottom of in-trays, and 'progress chasing' is necessary to make sure answers are received. People new to community action often know none of this (though they know many other things) and do not always appreciate the need to follow particular procedures. I once felt like a killjoy explaining to a group why it would be very difficult to overturn the policy that a Parks Department football pitch could not be hired on a Sunday. On the one hand, it is often better to explain such formalities in order to prepare people for the response they will probably get if they tackle the outside world in the 'wrong' way, rather than allowing them to go ahead and come back defeated. On the other hand, there is no substitute for people learning through direct experience that the way they want to do something will not work and that other avenues must be explored. The way to do this productively is to try to create situations where the group will learn not just that a particular approach will not work but why. In the above example, it might have been a good idea to get the parks superintendent to a meeting to explain the policy to the group rather than doing it myself.

Community groups may initially deal with the authorities inappropriately, sometimes with simple aggression, which may not produce the required results and may alienate councillors. Over time, however, most groups can be helped to learn how to deal effectively with power holders.

Professionals in groups

It can be problematic when a community group contains professionals such as housing workers or teachers. Professionals may not be good at understanding where local people are 'coming from' and may lack the patience and ability to explain, several times if necessary, how they see things and why they operate as they do. They may talk a different language, and they may also show a lack of respect for local people if they do not understand how a particular procedure operates. As a consequence, local people may feel inhibited.

On the other hand, the exchange which groups with 'outside professionals' in (or attending) them can create is sometimes very productive. Residents learn from professionals, for example, the problems of operating a refuse-collection service, and professionals learn from residents, in an immediate way, how people feel about community needs.

Sometimes professionals dominate community groups and impose their own agendas. If this happens and the professional does not respond to tactful hints, the worker may have to have a word with him or her privately. Many problems like this are best dealt with outside the group or through carefully prepared 'pre'-meetings between very small numbers of people. Sometimes groups themselves 'discipline' members who are creating problems, but this is difficult with high-status outsiders.

Work with existing groups

If you are asked to become involved in an existing group or you take the initiative to contact it, you may operate rather differently from the way in which you would work with a group which you started. Your role is likely to be limited. You may have been asked by the group for specific advice, on how to apply for a grant, for instance. Or you may have made contact with the group because you want to assist it to become more effective or because you have specific tasks in mind which you think it could take on.

It is easier to help a group strengthen its work in an area in which its members are already interested than to get them to change their focus. Also, where a group has asked you to help with a specific problem, it is relatively easy to say you are prepared to do A or B, but not D or E – that is, to establish an agreement about what you can offer over an agreed timescale. While we should aim to have such agreements with all groups, it is more difficult when we set up new ones because the members may not initially be ready for such an agreement to be made. We then have to convey what our role is more subtly. By contrast, the existing group will already be running itself, and so the worker will probably not be drawn into carrying out the myriad activities which are often necessary to help a new group get off the ground and stay alive.

Also, our relationship with groups which come into existence without our help is often not as intimate as with those which we help to create.

Working with moribund groups

Once, when I wanted to revive a particular tenants' association, I discovered that it existed in name only, and the secretary was the only member! This person was still committed to the association, and I decided to work with him to re-establish it. However, he was not popular, and his presence probably prevented other people from joining. I was concerned about hurting his feelings if I made no effort to involve him, so I partly involved him by telling him about meetings but doing most of the work with other individuals. However, I felt uneasy working in this way, probably because I had not fully made up my own mind what to do. In this kind of situation it is very important to think and consult with a colleague or your manager before you act.

When a group was declining I sometimes asked the members whether it should be disbanded. This normally resulted in people deciding to carry on, perhaps because they could not face the fact that the initiative had failed. In retrospect, I now believe that I should have tried to get them to explore the issue more seriously, examine different alternatives and perhaps to face some stark realities rather than simply asking the question.

If you believe that a group should disband, I think you should find the right time and then state that, in your view, the group should cease to exist, and explain why but also listen to arguments why it should not. You would then either withdraw or work, with the agreement of the existing members, to help it wind up.

A directive approach to setting up a group

Community workers are paid primarily to assist the development of community groups. But what happens if, after six months' work, no group emerges? Two workers tried to help gypsy families on an unofficial site organise to put their case to the authorities for the provision of basic facilities and to press for an official site. No organisation emerged after two years' work. The workers decided that, as group organisation seemed to be an alien method of approach for the gypsies, they, the workers, should set up some activities, including a literacy scheme and a summer play scheme, which they did. As well as providing needed services, their objective was, in part, to show the gypsies that something positive could be done, and thereby to engender within them the idea that they could act for themselves.

Playing this kind of leadership role can sometimes enhance the capability of people in the community to take action themselves. However, although our ultimate objective is that community members should run schemes themselves, they may never take them over if the worker runs them initially. Also, it is easy to deceive ourselves that it is really the people who are running the scheme (and we are only advising), whereas in reality they see us as the leader. When I set up an anti-motorway action group, which local people certainly wanted, I gathered people together and we started various actions, raising money in particular. Only when I discovered that I was doing all the work did I realise that, although I saw the group as theirs, they saw it as mine! They would follow if I led, but they would not lead. I later accepted this and led because 'product' in this situation was more important than 'process'.

Creating larger organisations and the need for professional staff

The tasks community groups take on often require a more sophisticated organisation than most disadvantaged communities are capable of creating. In many situations this results in the job still getting done but less successfully. The carnival is badly organised but still takes place, for example. In other situations poor organisation is a recipe for total disaster.

The example of a 'community association' will illustrate the problems and needs of larger organisations. Community associations in Britain are 'umbrella' organisations which bring together representatives from existing groups and sometimes statutory and other bodies, as well as representatives direct from the neighbourhood. Their purpose is to take up or promote a range of issues or activities, and these often include the management of a community centre. If a community association is to be set up the following questions need considering. Which groups and organisations should be asked to send a representative to the governing body? Do you want councillors? If so, should they have a vote? Do you want shopkeepers and industry? Do you want representatives from pubs, working-men's clubs, trades unions? What kind of representation should local authority departments have, if any? What about the status of professional workers in the area such as youth workers or clergy? Should individuals be allowed to join the governing body (which I will call a council)? How often should the council meet? Should you try to run everything through the council or should there be sub-committees: to run the newsletter, the carnival or the play scheme? How will such sub-committees differ in practice from similar but independent community groups constituting the organisation? How will their work be co-ordinated? If the council only meets every two months, how can important decisions be taken quickly? Do you need a smaller executive committee meeting which meets more frequently? How can an executive committee make sure that the council members do not feel they are just rubber-stamping decisions already taken? How will financial control be managed? Will the table tennis group have to get permission from the council to buy new balls? Should sub-committees spend the funds they raise or must they pay some or all to the central organisation? Who is to take the minutes and print and distribute them? How do you ensure that the various parts of the organisation communicate with each other? Does the organisation need equipment, a minibus, for example, and, if so, how will such resources be managed? Is the organisation so big that it needs to employ paid staff? If so, how will the resources be raised for this and how will the staff be managed? Is it necessary to register as a charity? Should there be individual subscriptions and, if so, how should these be collected? How do you get local people to participate in an organisation which has had to develop formal procedures in order to manage itself?

In large community organisations (at least those which are effective) five or six people, possibly fewer, will run the organisation between them. In theory, decisions are democratic. In reality they are often taken outside the formal meetings by one or two people who do most of the work. Making a large community organisation function effectively on an entirely voluntary basis over a long period of time in an area where there does not exist a great deal of organisational expertise generally requires the services of a community worker or similar professional. Although it is possible for the worker to withdraw, to an extent, from small community groups, it is often not possible to withdraw from a complex, multi-purpose organisation.

In theory, large organisations have more power than simpler community groups. In practice, however, this is not always the case, particularly with umbrella organisations composed of people representing a range of interests. Such an organisation will tend to move at the pace of the slowest or the most conservative, and it is much easier to prevent action being taken than to initiate it. Umbrella organisations which consist of the same type of constituent group (such as federations of tenants' associations) where there is considerable agreement both about the problems and the means by which to solve them are on occasion able to muster a considerable amount of power. However, even then one interest group can still dominate. In one large town a federation of tenants' associations was once established. But its key member associations concentrated on the problems of houses made of steel which were now corroding. The other constituent associations whose members lived in brick-built houses eventually left. If we are involved in setting up an umbrella organisation, we need to think about how to keep all groups involved.

The large complex community organisation has a tendency to become remote from its constituency. It can also act as a buffer between 'simpler' community groups and the authorities which may expect these always to go through the umbrella organisation. It is also difficult for members of an umbrella organisation to give time both to the community group (or groups) which they represent and to the umbrella organisation. This increases the likelihood that the umbrella organisation will be dominated by an out-of-touch clique. It requires vast amounts of community work time to ensure the links are kept between these constituent groups and the umbrella organisation.

If you are working with a complex community organisation you may find yourself acting rather like an employee, that is, implementing its decisions. You also need to think about whether you should attend the organisation as a member, which you may be eligible to do. It is, however, difficult to play the enabling role at the same time as one is acting as a member, particularly if one also has the job of secretary or any other office. If one is the secretary of a large organisation, there are many executive tasks to undertake which involve heart as well as head, and actions taken must sometimes be defended. Consequently it is often difficult to stand back and advise on the maintenance and future development of the organisation.

Withdrawal: from intensive work to 'servicing' to 'exit'

A common catchphrase is that community workers should make themselves redundant. However, while workers can and should withdraw from particular groups, often there will be other needs requiring their attention within the same area. In the long term they may be able to say that a particular community can take care of its own needs. But, with disadvantaged communities, withdrawal should probably never happen completely. This is because wider processes in society and the global economy create and perpetuate disadvantaged communities. Such communities will, therefore, need continuing support to organise themselves, particularly if those who have gained confidence and skill leave, to be replaced by other disadvantaged people. It was evident in the Duffryn Project (Thomas, 1997) that, when the community workers withdrew, the community-run groups and training courses which they had successfully established began to decline.

For a neighbourhood based worker it is possible to identify three types of withdrawal. These are:

1. withdrawal from an intensive role to a 'servicing' role;
2. withdrawal from a servicing role;
3. leaving that neighbourhood altogether.

However, the principles of withdrawal are very similar for each type.

Withdrawal is often handled badly, partly, perhaps, because of the emotional implications. It is likely that workers get some satisfaction from being in the centre of the action. They may not cope easily with the loss of status from being no longer centrally involved with a project. They may feel lost if a group is no longer dependent on them.

Many different forces are likely to influence your decision to withdraw: not only demands made on you from other areas of work but also, perhaps, your own feelings of frustration with a particular group. All these feelings can be uncomfortable, and it is often easier not to face them. But only if you deal with them can you withdraw in such a way as to benefit the group. The emotions of the group's members also need to be taken into account.

In the early stages of withdrawal, you are both carrying out your old role of servicing the group and probably training a group member or searching out another professional to take over certain of your functions. It takes a great effort to devote extra attention to the group when you have left it behind mentally and are reaching out to pastures new. It is during withdrawal, above all, that your policy of having an agreement with the group will pay off. If you have given the impression that you will be around for ever and that you are just an ordinary group member, you should not be surprised if the members are angry when you tell them you are leaving the next week! However, it will be easier if you have emphasised that your job is to help establish the group and then to move out, and if you discuss your role with the group from time to time.

There is also the question of when to withdraw. Ideally, the first consideration should be whether the group will decline or collapse without the worker although, in practice, the decision to withdraw may be affected by many other considerations. Judging when to withdraw is complicated by the fact that any worker reaches a point of diminishing returns. The initial period of intensive work, if successful, sees a marked development in the effectiveness of the group. But even if a worker continues to work intensively, the rate of improvement tends to slow down. It is likely, also, that your aspirations are for the group to achieve a higher level of functioning than is actually possible. When the group's growth in performance begins to level off you can either continue to work intensively with it or withdraw to a servicing role. If you withdraw to a servicing role there are two main scenarios. First, the group might continue in existence at more or less the same level of functioning. Secondly, it could die, either slowly or quickly. In deciding whether to withdraw, either completely or from an intensive role to a servicing role, you need to work out which of these (or other) scenarios is the most likely and plan accordingly.

When you are considering withdrawal it is normally within the context of other claims on your time. There will be other groups or projects with which you may be involved. Perhaps a group is starting somewhere else to which you could be of use, but you do not currently have the time to work with this new group. Certain kinds of groups will also have greater priority for you than others. If you have spent a considerable amount of effort setting up a mechanism whereby tenants' representatives meet regularly with housing officials, you will probably be unwilling to risk the death of this group. Consequently, you might never withdraw completely from it.

Community groups tend to spring up for a particular purpose and then decline and die. Sometimes, the desire among community workers to preserve groups at any cost may inhibit the formation of other groups. Alternatively, if one allows this natural process of birth, development, decline and death to take its course, the groups with which one is working may never reach the stage of dealing with complex matters, negotiating effectively or forming a partnership with major power holders. You must decide whether a particular group is likely to play a part in your future vision for the community, in which case you will probably be unwilling to let it die.

In reality, you may have to withdraw before a group can stand on its own feet and there will be nobody who can continue the work. In that case you should, if possible, help the group establish contact with a range of individuals who can offer help in specific areas. You could also try to link the group with similar groups, the members of which can sometimes offer advice and help. Given the frequently short-term nature of community work posts, a major role for all workers, from the start, should perhaps be to identify such support mechanisms and seeking to ensure that all the community groups with which they work use them. Such mechanisms can be difficult to find, however.

Inevitably the stages of withdrawal from intensive work through routine servicing to complete withdrawal tend to merge. When you are servicing rather than working intensively with a group, you may still attend some meetings. You may also provide limited services on an agreed basis. You will probably still have some contact with certain group members. But the group is less dependent on you. The onus of responsibility for your involvement has begun to shift from you to the group, and you need to ensure that the members understand this. It is now increasingly up to the group to ask for advice. The worker becomes less a teacher, more a consultant, reactive rather than 'pro-active'.

Once you have withdrawn to a routine servicing role you should be wary of becoming involved intensively again. Quite often a crisis would arise in a group just after I had withdrawn and I would feel pressure to take up my old role. Unless you withstand that pressure you may never succeed in withdrawing. When withdrawing you must also find ways of demonstrating that you still regard the group's work as important because, whatever people say, they may feel that they are being betrayed.

When you have withdrawn completely, you will probably wish to maintain a minimum of contact, perhaps by inviting the group to contact you in the future if the members think you could be of use. You might also attend the annual general meeting (if there is one) or occasionally telephone the chair to hear how the group is getting on.

When you move away from the neighbourhood the process of withdrawal is rather different. You may have to withdraw quite quickly from a group with which you have been working intensively, and that is difficult to do well. Ideally, we need to inform the people with whom we are working as early as possible that we are thinking of moving on so they can consider the implications. Then, when we have obtained another job, we should give ourselves plenty of time to withdraw decently. I found three months adequate, but it had to be talked through with care.

The closure of a whole project raises very similar issues which Simpson (1995b) describes with sensitivity and eloquence. In his project, closure was known about, accepted and planned for twelve months ahead. All the staff stayed until the end, the local authority had more or less agreed to take over some aspects of the work, and it worked well. But it was still difficult and time-consuming. Other projects may be closed down because the funder has withdrawn resources, perhaps suddenly, in a situation where some staff have already left, where those remaining are in conflict with each other and where, consequently, no real work is carried out for several months before the closedown. In that kind of situation morale is usually at rock bottom and there is probably no will to devise a good exit plan.

Simpson (1995b) lists the following points which should be taken into account when closing a project:

• Plan an exit strategy a year in advance.
• Alert others about the timescale.
• Seek to ensure the work you are undertaking is replaced by other support organisations.
• Withdraw gradually.
• Have the withdrawal strategy on a chalk board and refer to it in regular review meetings.
• Keep sponsors, management committee and community groups informed and, if possible, involved.
• Ensure, if possible, that an evaluation of the work is completed and made available.
• Consider what dissemination activities might be useful and carry them out.
• Ensure that proper staff redundancy procedures are understood and the time is taken to implement these with the necessary care.
• Agree the principles on which the disposal of assets will be decided before deciding their actual disposal (preferably in written form at the beginning of the project).

- Bear in mind that project closure can be a particularly painful process as the equipment in the project office starts disappearing before one's eyes!
- Make a list of what needs to be done, for example, about disconnecting telephones, winding up the photocopier lease, writing final letters of thanks, disposing of files, closing bank accounts, and what needs to be done when.

To conclude: the process of withdrawal is as critical as the initial stages of establishing a community work initiative. Plan it with care.

Contract work?

Ideally, perhaps, community groups should be able to engage community workers as consultants just as they might hire a lawyer or an architect. As community work becomes more established and community groups adopt sophisticated goals, this method of 'contract working' may develop. This kind of relationship between a community organisation and a support worker or agency is potentially important, since, in theory, it enables the dignity of the members of the group to be maintained in that they know what they are getting and can control it, at least to some degree, rather than being under the control of the worker (as tends to be the case in more conventional community work). See Hyatt and Skinner, 1997, for a thorough discussion of contract working.

Community capacity building

Over the last decade in Britain, and earlier in the US, a new (and, I think, little understood) phrase 'community capacity building' has become current.

In today's world, inexperienced local residents are increasingly required to participate in the design and implementation of regeneration strategies, sometimes costing millions of pounds. The concept of building the capacity of the communities to act effectively has grown up in this context. Skinner (1997) defines community capacity building primarily as:

development work that strengthens the ability of community organisations... to build their structures, systems, people and skills so that they are better able to define and achieve their objectives and engage in consultation and planning, manage community projects, and take part in partnerships and community enterprise. It includes aspects of training, organisational and personal development and resource building organised in a self-conscious manner reflecting the principles of empowerment and equality.

(pp.1–2)

Thus, capacity building includes a wide range of forms of learning as well as organisational change. (See also Armstrong, 1998, Nugent, 1998, and Nye, 1998, for other descriptions of approaches to capacity building.)

A major characteristic of effective capacity building work is that the community organisation has to 'own' the process. While the consultant or trainer works with the group to identify needs and structures the learning, he or she always needs to link this with the aims of the group or needs of its members. Capacity building is essentially guided learning through group-based activity.

Skinner also emphasises (pp. 64–84) the importance of the organisational development aspects of capacity building, which he believes many community workers do not adequately engage with. Here the focus is on strengthening the community organisation itself rather than just on the skill development of the individual members. The process may involve building effective team relationships, designing a constitution and establishing good communication and management systems as well as action plans. He also stresses the need to develop capacity-building plans based on reviews of individuals' training needs and the organisation's development needs.

In reality, some work which purports to be community capacity building is not clearly needs-based.

Community capacity building cannot be carried out at all if the group does not recognise the need for it, and it always has to be negotiated with the group first. Sadly, some of the organisations which profess to offer capacity-building assistance to community groups do not appreciate the need for this vital prerequisite and do not have the attitudes and skills necessary to carry it out. Capacity

building should also, argues Skinner, focus on creating or strengthening the community infrastructure, which community organisations also need. This consists of: providing resources (for example,
printing equipment), improving opportunities for networking,
creating participative structures, ensuring community development
support is provided and building the capacity of professional organisations (pp. 85–104).

As community participation and work to promote it become
more central to public policy (discussed in Chapter 8) the skills of
capacity building will, in my view, be increasingly in demand.

One key element of capacity building is training. However, community group members can be reluctant to participate in training
courses, even when run in their own centres. This may be because
they have had bad experiences at school, be barely literate and
afraid to reveal this or merely unaware of the gaps in their knowledge and skill. I have known many occasions when a training
course was arranged for the members of a community group and
nobody came. Simpson (1995a) argues that successful training for
community groups can normally only be provided if it arises from
and is followed by community development work. Trainers who are
merely interested in getting their subject across or ensuring the
'trainees' gain qualifications rarely make good trainers for community groups.

A prior understanding of 'where the group is at' is needed and,
even then, trainers may have to adapt their material substantially if
it does not fit with what the group members are ready for. One such
trainer discovered that the local mums, who had been successfully
encouraged by a community worker to come to his introductory
course on word-processing, were so scared of computers that he
decided not even to switch one on during the first evening! Instead,
he just chatted, building trust with the women, about their school
experiences, the nature of the playgroups they were running and
voluntary work they were doing, why they thought computer skills
might be useful, and so on. The next week they were happy for him
to start the course.

If the right kind of relationship is developed by the trainer and if
the content of the training is negotiated in an unthreatening way,
then confidence builds, and the participants will be more open to
becoming involved in the training. This type of preparation is a key
contribution which community work can make to capacity building.

The most successful courses are often those where experiential learning, small group exercises, guided visits and so on are used. A training course for community groups should also be evaluated afterwards. Finally, care needs to be given to devising appropriate arrangements for those with caring responsibilities, and to covering transport and other out-of-pocket expenses.

It often seems to be the case today that women are more interested in training than men, and I have sometimes noticed the following sequence occurring. First, women become interested in running local ventures, such as playgroups. Then, they begin to realise that they need education and training to develop their work more effectively, and they ask for non-vocational courses. Next they see the need for vocational qualifications and are prepared to register for these too. Finally, some of the men become interested!

The training needs of community groups and their members vary from committee skills to business plans, from how to supervise staff to how to recruit volunteers, from how to manage a building, to how to keep accounts, and many more. By starting from the needs both of the individual and of the community organisation, and by using a carefully chosen range of learning methods, many of the blocks to involvement in capacity building can be overcome. Only as people find that they benefit from training do they develop a 'love of learning' and become more prepared to attend conventional courses.

Community capacity building has great potential to act as a bridge to enable communities to become more involved in projects, programmes and partnerships. It needs to become, and is to a degree becoming, a crucial element in economic and social regeneration as public agencies increase their openness to joint working at community level.

4
Working with Community Groups II: Dealing with Practical Issues and Problems

Participation in community action

Why do people participate?

People participate for what *they* get out of it. If community workers want to avoid frustration they should not expect people, including their colleagues, to be very altruistic. You might work for two years with little success trying to organise a group to take up a range of environmental issues. Then a minor newspaper article suggests some waste land may be used as a gypsy site. Overnight an organisation forms in the same area and quickly organises a twenty-four-hour picket!

The basis for bringing people together is self-interest. Even if people are altruistically motivated, which many of course are, personal interest will probably dictate their area of involvement. One of our first jobs is to understand their motivation and self-interest.

Factors preventing participation

Sociological analysis has emphasised divisions of class, gender and race. There are, however, many more subtle differences between groups of people which can also be significant – for instance, Jamaicans might prefer not to mix with Barbadians – and a community worker needs to understand such differences.

If the first people who are recruited or who select themselves for a particular community activity are from one 'sub group', (the 'roughs', for instance), the 'respectables' will not come and vice versa. Whatever activity is started it will quickly attract an image which, in effect, prevents other people from participating. In addition, people often think of their 'home area' as very local, encompassing only a few streets, and, perhaps for that reason, it is common for meetings of community groups to be attended only by people who live less than a quarter of a mile from the meeting place. Several of them will already know each other and some may well be related. All these factors inhibit wider attendance at meetings and tend to increase the cliquishness of a group.

All the members of a community may share the same problem at a general level but may want different solutions. For some people in bad housing improvement means a transfer but for others it means refurbishing existing property. Even when the objective is clear, people differ as to how it should be achieved. The differences are often so great as to ensure that only those whose methods are adopted stay in the group.

The forces keeping people in community groups are relatively weak. Even the most committed members are generally more concerned about their personal and work lives than about their community activity, and we must all cope with illness, childbirth, bereavement and so on. During a crisis which occurred between two bingo-group leaders with whom I worked, one of them was also about to be evicted for non-payment of rent which, as would be expected, took precedence over her community concerns. Nevertheless, for some people the community group can assume an importance which may seem somewhat out of proportion. For example, the chair of a disabled club once told me he had spent two successive nights awake trying to work out the cheapest arrangements for an outing for the members.

How far do the poor participate?

There is some evidence that really poor, deprived or oppressed people (especially women) may join together in collective action if the situation is bad enough (see, for example, Gallagher, 1977). But if the situation is not too severe the worker may have to work very slowly, initially by arranging social activities, for example, gradually building up their motivation and confidence.

Vertical participation

Participation by ordinary people in activities run by the community itself is sometimes called horizontal participation. Participation in programmes which are primarily the responsibility of government can be seen as vertical participation. Some examples are community regeneration boards, community health councils, tenant consultative committees and parent representation on the managing bodies of schools. There are, however, several different levels of vertical participation. At the 'lowest' level, government merely informs a community, about the closing of a road, for instance. At 'higher' levels, vertical participation involves consultation prior to a decision being taken, and joint action and devolved power where the community makes its own decisions on a particular matter.

Vertical participation is problematic, both because government often purports to consult when it really wants to get support for what *it* wants to do and because community groups mostly want, and sometimes think they have got, devolved power when they are merely being consulted or even informed. While effective vertical participation is vital in a democracy, you need to think clearly when involving community groups in this because they can be used merely to legitimate decisions which would have been taken anyway and which may not be in the community's interest.

Understanding and influencing group processes

Helping groups to make decisions

Community groups often find it difficult to take decisions. I have been to many meetings where hours have been spent discussing matters such as whether new coffee cups should be bought. One reason for this is that in some groups the members unconsciously hope to take every decision by consensus. One way to help a group to deal with this is to encourage members to vote occasionally.

Also, groups sometimes take decisions in such a clumsy way that misunderstandings occur. The carnival committee discussed making a grant of £10 to another organisation but decided, I thought, to defer the matter until the next week. At the next meeting the matter was not mentioned until a member raised it, only to find that the treasurer, thinking the decision had already been taken, had already paid over the money! You need to anticipate such problems and, perhaps, to intervene to ensure that everyone knows the decision, particularly if minutes of meetings are not kept.

On the other hand, when an important item comes up unexpectedly, it is often a good idea to try to have the decision deferred to another meeting, when people will have had time to think about it. Otherwise a decision may be taken hurriedly which the members will regret.

There will be other occasions when a group continually postpones a difficult decision, and you may have to work both with individuals and with the group as a whole to help the members face it.

Remember, too, that people do not always act logically, at least as far as the logic of the worker is concerned. Let us say, for example, that the chair takes the minutes of meetings. A suggestion that there should be a separate minutes secretary, which would be in the chair's own interest, might well be rejected by them because it could be perceived as a criticism.

Many needs are met in groups which are not to do with the stated aims of the group. If the stated aim, to run a carnival, for example, requires a meeting once a month but the group is meeting weekly, the reason may be that the more frequent meetings meet expressive needs, which even the members do not recognise. When working with any group, workers can usefully ask themselves which needs it is meeting and for whom, since meeting the unstated needs of some members is likely to cause frustration for others.

You need to be aware of the ways in which community groups tend to behave and find ways of intervening appropriately. This is not always easy. In some cases, in a particularly emotive meeting, for instance, you may find it difficult to get a word in at all. One way to deal with this is to mention to the chair beforehand that there is a particular point you want to raise.

Finally, if a group does not accept an idea from the worker at one point, this does not necessarily mean the members have forgotten about it. We should be patient and continue 'sowing seeds'. We never know when they will bear fruit.

Making meetings work

Few people will attend meetings regularly which go on after 10 p.m., and, as the members have come to see business done, they will not be satisfied if the meeting does not complete this business reasonably efficiently. So, if possible, meetings should be kept reasonably short. But the thoughts of members often do not coincide with items on the agenda: they might prefer to speak of a personal experience or tell a joke. Some allowance should be made for people to express these feelings, and some community workers are excellent at facilitating such informal interchange. If these expressive needs are not satisfied, the decision-making process may feel rather sterile. Also, if people are prevented from expressing their emotions in the group, they may express them in some other way, for example, in unreasoned opposition to a sensible proposal purely because it was made by a certain person. However, meeting expressive needs may conflict with effective decision taking. Some group members are good at ensuring tasks are effectively undertaken; others are better at taking care of 'socio-emotional' needs. The worker has to try to promote the right balance (and be human at the same time!).

It is good if you can find some tasks for the group which are fun and easy to do, since groups often begin to 'gel' when the members work together. One occasion which was enjoyed by all participants was when the carnival committee spent several evenings turning two roomfuls of groceries into 1,200 Christmas parcels for old people!

However, groups often concentrate on the tasks they enjoy rather than what they 'ought' to be doing. They may also change their objectives without fully realising it. The carnival committee began with the purpose of running a carnival but found that it made money, most of which was distributed in kind to pensioners. Later, the committee members spoke as if the rationale for the carnival was to raise money for pensioners. The role of the worker here might be to help members see what is happening and decide if this is what they want.

Over-involvement

A volunteer may become so involved in a particular activity, a youth club, say, that they open it every night of the week, find that they cannot cope, and have to reduce it to one day, thus creating frustration and aggression in the young people. Emotionally over-involved people are to a large degree meeting their own needs and, when problems arise, they are likely to react as if they had been personally insulted, blaming the people for whose benefit they are supposed to be working. The enthusiasm turns to a sense of martyr-dom, and often the person gives up. It is not easy to prevent people from getting over-involved. But be prepared for it and the likely consequences.

Keeping calm

Another emotional reaction which the worker has to guard against is panic. When groups organise events – public meetings or exhib-itions, for example – crises sometimes occur in particular combin-ations. The man providing transport for the older participants does not arrive, but Jane is going that way to collect the ice cream and agrees to do the job. Then she finds she has to go to the other side of town and forgets to collect the older people. The temptation during such crises is to rush round madly, which often creates more crises. In such situations we can have a calming effect on others if we can appear calm. Similarly, if you speak confidently, even if you do not feel it, you will raise the confidence of those around you. Whatever the mood of the group, depressed or over-confident, it is important for community workers to maintain a degree of objectivity and to use their relationship with the group to create balance.

Perceptions

We have to be aware of how other people perceive us. Our commu-nity work office also ran an advice centre. Consequently, we became tagged with a 'welfare' label as a result of which some residents refused to come to our building. Because, as a community worker, I succeeded a 'motherly', female worker, some of the women with whom she had worked became quite resentful that I was not prepared to give them the same attention as she had done. To find out how we are seen we need to keep our eyes and ears open and also to develop a range of contacts whom we can ask for feedback.

Building confidence

Our presence may have a symbolic value for people. The fact that I
was *their* worker and the neighbourhood centre was *their* project
probably helped several people in the neighbourhood to feel that
someone cared about them after all. Dora, for example, never came
to our advice centre, but I was told she kept a list of our opening
times in her purse. One effect created by the newsletter which we ran
was a feeling of pride among some residents that their estate had a
newsletter while others did not. We ignore at our peril these intangible aspects of our work, because what goes on in people's heads
can make the difference between success and failure (see Goleman,
1996).

Mistakes and failure

For some months we had been trying to establish better relationships between our council housing estate and the neighbouring
estate. The adventure playground was due to be moved from the
middle of our estate to a new site between the two estates. We had
done some door-knocking on the neighbouring estate to tell
people it was coming (informing, not consulting!), but this was
not very thorough. When residents there opposed the move, I
tried to retrieve the situation by spending time with the key
protester. I admitted that we were at fault since we had not
discussed the matter with her community earlier, and I told her
how she could oppose the move of the playground, at the same
time saying that, as I was the chair of the playground, I could not
support her.

When we have made a mistake we can often go some way to
retrieving the situation, but we normally have to start by admitting
our error. We are likely to have fewer problems in the long run if we
are as honest as possible in this respect.

Because community work is not an exact science we will often
fail in our objectives. The skill is not to never make mistakes
or fail but to know how to deal with such occurrences
effectively, learn from them and start again. You also have to be
able to handle uncertainty well to be an effective community
worker.

Dealing with conflict

Certain problems, particularly deep-seated conflicts between individuals, are rarely resolved easily, and it is often not worth trying. However, some workers have managed to help groups overcome such difficulties. A worker with a group of tenants living in appalling accommodation found that personality differences between members were jeopardising the group's survival. He confronted the group and pointed out that if the members continued to disagree violently they would never succeed in their campaign. His point was eventually accepted, and the inter-personal conflict subsided somewhat. But he had a very high status in the group, and the members were strongly motivated.

The inevitable prominence of certain community leaders often generates a mixture of negative feelings among other group members. Indeed, any community activity may arouse some antagonism, perhaps because many of us are sometimes a little jealous of others and do not like to see them succeed. Some community leaders heighten antagonism by making sure that it is always their photograph which appears in the paper, for instance. We must be careful not to fan smouldering jealousies.

When people are strongly committed to their group, strong emotions can be aroused. People can also feel vulnerable in groups, but groups can also be enormously supportive. Two bingo-group leaders once had a vicious argument in another committee over a trivial matter. The real issue was that they each saw the other as a threat. Subsequently, one of them telephoned the police to say that the other was running bingo illegally. There is no prescription for action in this kind of situation except: think carefully before you intervene.

At some stage most workers have to deal with personal hostility from community members, councillors, or officials. Most people deal with it instinctively, either by hitting back or by trying to conciliate. In my view it is generally advisable not to lose one's temper, to consider whether there is anything in the criticism which is deserved and to apologise for that if it is appropriate to do so, explaining one's position calmly. However, at times it can be appropriate to 'allow oneself' to get angry. If done rarely and with good reason, losing your temper can be very effective in getting what you want.

All community workers should be able to apply the principles of assertiveness. Once, when I was taken to task by two of my colleagues about failing to discuss a proposed project with them, part of me felt under personal attack. But in order to respond effectively I had to keep those feelings down and deal with the issue calmly and intelligently. (See Chapter 9 for more on assertiveness.)

Another useful way of dealing with situations involving personal criticism of you is to listen carefully to what is being said by the other party and to say you will let them have your response later when you have had time to think about it calmly.

Conflict is often, and self-evidently, a stimulus for change. A community organisation may be run by an out-of-touch clique which has no concern for the wider community. Changing that situation involves conflict, and the worker's task might be to work with newer members to build up their confidence so that they will challenge the old guard. Or, the worker might try to bring the conflict into the open in the group. The degree to which a worker can do this successfully may well depend upon the nature of their 'contract' with the group. Remember, however, that people mostly avoid conflict if they can. An agreement made by a group member, prior to a meeting, to raise an issue in the group might amount to nothing in practice if it meant challenging the leadership.

When people living in poor circumstances come together for the first time the anger expressed against the most likely target – usually the authorities but sometimes it can be the worker or one of their own number – can be considerable. Be prepared for this; help them articulate their discontent and work through it. It is often a necessary step on the way to effective action. Beware, however, of people who are constantly critical of others. They can be very difficult to work with and may become critical of you at a later stage.

When community groups first attempt to pressurise the authorities to change a policy or procedure, the 'other side' often overreacts. Councillors and officials may become angry and try to pressurise the group to give up (perhaps via the community worker – especially if he or she is a local authority employee). During such times the group members may require considerable support. But if groups can be helped to persevere, the authorities sometimes come to accept that the group is working in a particular way, and stop over-reacting. In the long run, they may even recognise that the group is doing a useful job and accept a certain amount of conflict. However, conflict between a community and a local authority can also cause resentment lasting decades. People have long memories.

Another difficult situation for the worker is where the community group is led by bigoted community members and the community worker's sympathy actually lies with the authorities. It is difficult to be prescriptive: I can only suggest that you think carefully about your role in such a situation and explain to the group, with respect, what your position is. We do not have to support a group at all costs.

We need to try to keep good relationships with people with whom we may be in conflict. The social services department had taken longer than a month to visit a client whom we had referred, and we decided to make a formal complaint. We were on friendly terms with the staff about whom we would be complaining and did not want them to feel we were attacking them. Consequently, I telephoned the senior social worker, explained our concern and said that we were writing in about it. She did not like the fact that we were complaining but was grateful to have been informed and continued to co-operate with us on other matters.

Dealing with prejudice

It is difficult to know what to do if the people we work with make what we consider to be prejudiced statements about 'problem families', immigrants, itinerants and other minority groups. I once heard an experienced community relations worker explain what she did. She used to say to white groups something like, 'I hear you hate blacks. Let's hear about it.' After a stunned silence the floodgates would burst open and many extreme statements would be made. But there were always one or two people in the group who might say, 'but they've got to live somewhere', and at that point she was able to get the group discussing more rationally. I would feel uneasy acting in this way, but this worker certainly went out of her way to recognise the feelings of the group.

On the one hand, oppressive statements can be challenged. On the other, silence can also communicate disapproval. Also, if you do not know how to respond at the time, you can think about it and raise the matter later. Or, rather than getting into a long argument about the rights and wrongs of the situation you can say something like

'...*I* don't like to hear remarks like...' (see also Chapter 7 for guidelines on anti-discriminatory practice).

Manipulation

Within any relationship manipulation can occur. At the beginning of a meeting with housing officials, a housing management assistant paid a compliment to one of the residents. That resident told me later that she felt this inhibited her from criticising the housing department in the meeting.

Ernie had let it be known that he was thinking of resigning from a particular committee. Fred, knowing I was in contact with Ernie, told me that he and the treasurer would resign if Ernie did, his unstated objective being to get me to prevent Ernie from resigning. Because emotional factors are brought to bear, such pressure can sometimes be difficult to resist, but the best response is either a carefully thought-out one or no response at all.

A counselling role?

The question of how far a community worker should offer counselling help to community members is difficult, particularly if you are a new worker who is trying to establish rapport. When you find that the only problems some people are prepared to talk about are personal, you can find you are assuming the role of social worker. The main role of a community worker with individuals is to help them learn how to undertake work for community benefit, which is different from helping somebody resolve personal difficulties. Nevertheless, there are times when it is reasonable to act as a counsellor, especially with residents with whom you are already closely involved and who seek your help in a crisis.

Learning by doing and getting groups to evaluate

Community groups learn by doing, which involves making mistakes. Sometimes when groups make mistakes, the lessons are obvious and the members change their behaviour, but not always. The need for a change in behaviour may be so threatening that the members are afraid to look at their mistakes. So they invent all sorts of rationalisations to explain them away. Community workers need to try to get the group to stand back and evaluate its achievements. Goetschius (1969, pp. 106–11), who has a useful section on helping a group to evaluate its work, comments that it is not enough merely to identify the mistakes. The members then have to decide how to alter their behaviour if they are to avoid repeating them.

When something which a worker predicted would go wrong does go wrong the worker needs to check out, in a calm atmosphere, whether the group members now understand how to avoid making the same mistake again. But do not expect the members to say you were right after all. Your satisfaction must be in seeing the changed behaviour.

I always found it difficult to get a group to evaluate and cannot make any clear recommendation in this respect. Ideally, I think, a worker should seek to agree with a group that periodic reviews will be undertaken. Without such an agreement you may have to use other methods. For instance, you may see that the group is not effective because Jack is doing all the work without prior approval by the committee. You might then raise this either in the group or with individuals. If you have a good relationship with the group and if the commitment of Jack and the other members is high, they may be prepared to collaborate to solve the problem. But if commitment is not high, you may create friction to no avail. You might, therefore, have to restrict your role to making minor practical suggestions.

Today the growing emphasis on evaluation in British community work, together with the emphasis in 'capacity building' on contracts and reviews, should make it easier for community groups to understand the importance of evaluation.

Using the media

It is sometimes important for groups to get publicity, particularly in the local paper, in order to boost the confidence of their members, to attract new members or to mobilise support. However, even if reporters have been invited to an event, they may not attend. Or they may highlight a minor remark, making it seem as if the group is criticising the council when it is not. Reporters also often try to talk to people who they consider will be articulate, such as community workers. However, they can gradually be 'trained' to talk to local people.

If community group members talk to the press they may need briefing beforehand. For example, the chair of a parent-teacher association who was interviewed on the day of a well-attended fête criticised the community for lack of support, and his words appeared as a headline the next day!

In order to control the information you give the press, it is often useful to have a short press release prepared. You can also take this, plus a photograph, to the local newspaper office. However, a story has to be presented in such a way as to be newsworthy. It pays also to establish contact with the news editor, some time prior to major events taking place, who will provide advice on how to get the best coverage. Remember, too, to supply newspapers with regular items of local (good) news which may prevent them from printing articles which negatively stereotype the area.

With local radio, the problems lie in being adequately prepared for a variety of questions and in giving local people the confidence to use this medium. While people mostly become used to speaking on the radio fairly quickly, they may need support or encouragement to start with. There are now a number of simple handbooks on this subject. There are also training courses on public speaking and media presentation which can sometimes be helpful.

Managing money

Allegations of financial mismanagement cause enormous antagonism within community groups. Therefore, community workers need to ensure that the members are aware of their financial responsibilities. We may not be too bothered personally if we find out that the treasurer of the tenants' association is keeping accounts on the back of a cigarette packet! But we would be worried if we discovered that the books did not balance and the rest of the committee was accusing them of embezzlement! While my work with community groups was mostly 'non-directive', I eventually became quite directive about account keeping, especially when activities involving cash were taking place on premises for which I was responsible. Treasurers should know how to keep proper accounts *before* things go wrong, as it is then often too late to rectify the situation. Again, there are several handbooks which cover this field. Or get a book-keeper's advice.

The law

The police once called at our neighbourhood centre and greeted me with the words 'We believe you have illegal gaming going on in these premises!' The bingo group had been giving money prizes for which we had no licence!

The law impinges on community work in many ways, from the need to obtain planning permission for a change of building use, to the laws relating to demonstrations and employment. It pays, therefore, always to consider the legal implications of any project in advance. While mastering seemingly bureaucratic legal requirements can seem to be an unnecessary chore, this is yet another area which we neglect at our peril.

Relationships with politicians

A friendly councillor is usually a great help to a community group, while an unsympathetic one can be enormously obstructive. However, a majority of councillors need to vote at the council meeting in order to bring about a change in a local authority policy or procedure and to allocate resources. Therefore a community group must be able to convince councillors that the decision should go in its favour. Notwithstanding the low poll at local elections, most local politicians place great store on the fact that they were elected. Consequently many are suspicious of community organisations which have no similar mandate. They often see community workers as a threat because we are involved in supporting activity which may challenge the council, and they sometimes react negatively to pressure from 'unrepresentative' community groups. Or, they may pay lip-service to community participation but speak against it in private. Although community groups are sometimes involved in disagreements with councillors, care must be taken not to alienate them unnecessarily.

Close contact with community groups and community workers can help councillors better understand the needs and perspectives of people at local level and, therefore, to argue their case better in the council. But any councillor will have other pressures, from officers, from their party, and from central government. Consequently, they will not always be able to represent the interests of the community group effectively in the council. There is a particular danger, however, with friendly councillors. If they give help to a group, its members may too readily accept the situation when the councillor says that nothing can be done. The group should still make its own representations to the council rather than relying entirely on the councillor. Workers also need to ensure as far as possible that councillors are not part of the community group but attend meetings, or parts of meetings, clearly in their councillor role. This is not always easy, particularly if they are also local residents.

In Britain, today, local authorities have to collaborate with a wide range of other organisations (public, community, private) to seek solutions to complex problems, just as councillors now need to work with officers to identify possible solutions to seemingly untractable problems in conditions of considerable uncertainty. The need to work in such ways is not always well understood by councillors, and community workers potentially have an important role in assisting them to see how more consultative ways of working can assist both them and the local community. Well organised communities can also assist the council in bids for central government funds.

Members of Parliament (MPs) are more remote than councillors, but they can sometimes intervene to good effect in local matters. A letter from an MP to the leader of the council, particularly if it draws attention to a procedure which had not been properly followed, can sometimes ensure that a case is re- examined, for instance.

It is important to try to establish relationships with potential councillors or MPs before they are elected or in power. It is more difficult later.

Personal politics

How far should we allow our own party political affiliation, if we have one, to be evident in our professional work? My view is that if community groups become *perceived* as pursuing party political goals, and if workers become *perceived* as party agents in disguise either by our managers or by elected representatives, we are likely to receive less co-operation from council officials and from councillors in general (not merely from those in opposing parties), and will find it more difficult to obtain our objectives. As Alinsky once said, 'You may be a vegetarian, but you will have to work with butchers, so keep quiet about it.' Community work can be legitimately described in a variety of ways to fit in with the major political ideologies, and it is usually possible to 'sell' it in terms which are acceptable to most political parties.

Living in the area

Should community workers live in the area in which they work? This question is complex and requires careful consideration in each case. The geographical areas in which community workers operate differ in size and homogeneity. If a worker is working across one district within a county it may be convenient and desirable to live in the area. Also, living in, say, a one-class housing estate can have its advantages. You make contacts easily. You appreciate the needs of other residents, who also identify with you because, to a degree, you are one of them. However, whenever you are at home or going about your personal business in the area, you are also, in a sense, 'at work', and you may not be able to relax or find the space to write reports, for instance. There is also the danger, when deeply involved in day-to-day work, of losing the objectivity necessary for good practice and failing to stand back and reflect. Therefore, workers should do whatever they feel able to do. They should not feel guilty about not living in the area if they think they can survive better by living outside it.

When I was a fieldworker I lived for a time with my wife (who was not employed as a community worker) in a council house which served also as office, advice centre, and meeting place for groups. In this situation a worker can feel guilty if he is upstairs watching television and a group is meeting downstairs without him. What does he do when he is ill? People call at all hours, often on trivial matters, and this can be difficult to tolerate for long. The pressures on a partner can also be considerable. We moved out after two years but I continued working there. I do not think the work suffered as a result.

The paradox of buildings

Community groups need places to meet, but their members need to understand the effort required to manage a community building. In particular, they have to consider ways of running it without sacrificing other activities. Similarly, if you have responsibility for managing even a small building, this may take you a minimum of one day per week: cleaning and caretaking must be arranged, wages paid, and a booking schedule organised. If the building is used for multiple purposes, there may be conflict between the various interests. If a disturbance is caused, neighbours may have to be placated. The creation of a user committee can sometimes help, and often some of these tasks can be delegated to a caretaker. But it still takes some time to liaise with the user groups and to manage the caretaker. Some community buildings have bars, and this area can also be a minefield.

Community Matters, the London based UK wide federation of community associations, many of whose members run buildings, has a range of short guides on such subjects.

Community groups often seem to make it a central purpose to acquire as large a community centre as possible, either newly built or as a refurbished chapel, redundant school or workmen's club. Such groups almost never fully investigate the running costs or work out where these will come from, and some such buildings close a few years later. Community workers need to figure out ways of ensuring that groups understand the problems they are likely to face should they obtain a building. Nevertheless, with adequate help, community groups can sometimes run community buildings more effectively than local authorities.

Community groups and self-funding

Community groups are sometimes expected to become self-funding, particularly if they have a community building. This aim is, in every case I have met, unrealistic. However, with a proper business orientation, which need not be in conflict with philanthropic goals, a group with an appropriate building could raise a greater proportion of its running costs, say 30 per cent rather than 10 per cent. Ways need to be found of helping groups acquire such expertise.

Advice centres and 'community houses'

Some community workers think that a good way to initiate community involvement is to set up an advice centre, on the assumption either that residents will run the service or that individual advice work will generate collective action. But these things do not always happen. When setting up an advice service you are acting as an initiator, not an enabler. You will need to be in the building during opening hours, which must be closely adhered to if you are to establish credibility. Consequently you cannot be working outside the building at the same time. Advice work is a semi-profession in its own right and, for every hour the centre is open, you will have to spend another hour collecting information, keeping up to date on legislation and taking further action on some individual cases. This will all detract from work with community groups; although, if the advice work is resourced properly, it can link in with other work by bringing you into contact with more people.

There are also other issues to consider. How does a worker in such a centre generate a free and easy atmosphere, involve residents in helping each other and, at the same time, preserve confidentiality? Some such centres are 'drop-in' places where people are encouraged to stay as long as they like. This approach can be excellent but it also has disadvantages. Some people may become upset because they feel that certain individuals are monopolising the place, for example. You also run the risk of losing sight of your objectives. You may feel you are doing useful work just because you are in contact with people all day, without working out what you are trying to achieve.

In spite of these difficulties, advice work plays an important part in some community projects and represents one of the successful innovations closely connected with community work. See Astin (1979) and Jerry Smith (1979) for two thoughtful accounts of some of the problems mentioned here.

Sometimes 'community houses' are provided, especially on council housing estates, for community groups to meet in. While these can work well, they can be problematic if they are not managed responsibly and are not adequately resourced.

Information and communication technology (ICT)

I once visited a resource centre in a rural community which had many computers for community use. The manager said with some pride that the centre was well used. When I asked him what was used most of all, he pointed to the photocopier! It turned out that practically no one used the computers! To be fair, ICT has helped many 'excluded' people gain information, contacts, confidence and skills. However, we need to remember that for probably most 'excluded' people it is the nature of the relationships they have with friends, outreach workers or other professionals which enables them to move into the 'acting community' and utilise any available equipment. The relationships make the technology 'user friendly'. The availability of the equipment alone will not encourage many 'excluded' people to access it.

The value and effects of work with community groups

Being involved in community action can help some people grow enormously and lead enriched lives, benefiting not only their family life but also their career. Community activists sometimes go on to become councillors and professionals, for instance. There are numerous other examples: for instance, the woman who for the last four years of her life was the secretary of a self-help group for disabled people and who, by her own account, was happier than she had been during the previous ten years, in spite of increasing pain. Also, there is now mounting evidence that people who are part of strong networks have less heart disease and generally recover more quickly from highly stressful situations such as train accidents than those who do not (see, for instance, McTaggart, 1998).

However, the direct positive effects from engaging in community action seem only to occur to small numbers of people. In addition, people often lose money by being involved in community groups; they take unpaid leave or subsidise the group, for instance. Often the only way to run a group successfully is to work intensively at it, and this sometimes causes breakdowns and marital stress. Another consideration is that being involved in community action often causes a person to look at the world in a new way – for example, a woman beginning to question her role as wife and mother – an important but sometimes traumatic process.

When people initiate a project, it is likely that they got the idea from someone else. Community work and community action help to spread the idea by demonstration that people can become involved in doing things themselves. People who are involved in community action probably also provide models for their children, who later become involved in similar activities, just as elected representatives often have parents who were on the council. However, these changes are often indirect, long-term and difficult to measure.

A linked point is that no one piece of community action should be viewed in isolation. Several years' work had been undertaken by my predecessor to help establish the carnival committee, within which were several able community leaders. By the time of my arrival, some of these leaders were aware that many other community needs required attention. I encouraged them to think about these, and two of them subsequently became leaders of other community groups and left the carnival committee, which declined somewhat. In encouraging these leaders I had probably contributed to the decline of the carnival, which I had not anticipated.

A certain local authority had planned a major road scheme to run through an inner-city area, demolishing several houses. When the bulldozers moved in, about a year after the public enquiry, and after several houses had already been compulsorily purchased, residents formed an action group to oppose the scheme. But by then there was no chance of stopping it. I raise this point not because I believe we should never become involved in a campaign we cannot win, but because workers sometimes dissipate their energies in such battles arousing expectations which cannot be met, while neglecting other tasks which might prove more fruitful.

Community groups can and do achieve significant objectives. But these changes are often more limited than the members hope they will be, and many groups die before achieving their stated objectives. A dispassionate analyst would probably conclude, not only that the efforts put in far exceed the concrete achievements, but also that not many members of community groups develop personally either. But are there other achievements and why is it that community workers feel so strongly that collective action is good? One answer is as follows. There are often some positive outcomes which are not intended and which are not connected in the minds of most people with the existence of a particular group. Jim became chairman of the parent-teacher association (PTA). At the same time, two students doing practical work with me started a youth club and, when they were due to depart, they found that he was willing to take over. He later started running a junior football team too. The PTA had provided a way in for him, first to fulfil himself more, and second to contribute to the community.

Community development work encourages at least some people to develop more confidence and a better self image, to take positive action and to believe that they can act, that they can cause positive change. Of the lessons learned by the participants in community action, perhaps the most important are new attitudes, new political perspectives and a broader understanding of how the world works. Grace, a single parent and community leader, told me that, since our project had been running, she had learned to stand her ground with the housing management assistant and no longer let her walk into the house at will. The carnival committee ran a reasonable carnival for a few years, as a result of which the area appeared on the front page of the local paper for positive reasons rather than because it was a 'debtors' haven'. This must have done a great deal to boost the self-esteem of residents.

Pressure from community groups alone does not seem to induce a governmental organisation to change a policy completely, though such pressure can help to modify governmental policies, especially if community groups forge alliances with other organisations which have greater influence. But community groups also have a longer term effect. Through running playgroups for thirty years or so in Britain, the pre-school playgroup movement was influential in affecting thinking about play. Also, campaigns against damp in council housing and campaigns for more women's refuges, though often unsuccessful in individual cases, have resulted in a recognition that certain types of house construction are faulty, and that there is an enormous amount of domestic violence. Similarly, the incorporation of equal opportunities policies in many organisations and to some extent in law, in Britain, has been the consequence, in particular, of campaigns from the women's and black movements. The major outcomes of community action are often the long-term effects on the climate of opinion and on subsequent legislation or service provision rather than their immediate concrete results. There is, however, a desperate need for good long-term research into the effects of community work and community action. In the absence of this, however, it is the faith of the community worker that our work is of value which must often sustain us, because concrete achievements may not.

5

Social Planning Approaches to Community Work

Introduction

While the uniqueness of community work lies in the 'community development' approach, what I term the 'social planning' approach is also vital. Today, this approach is perhaps more common than the community development approach, since workers are often employed to seek the benefit of a particular group or community, but not, necessarily, to encourage its members to organise themselves to seek their own benefit.

Social planning 'proper' encompasses many activities, such as economic planning, health service planning, transport planning, and so on, which have little to do with community work. Thus, since most people who engage in social planning could not be described as community workers, the term 'social planning' within community work needs careful defining.

Community workers undertake many activities other than assisting community groups to run their own activities or projects. These can range from doing minor things *for* groups all the way to planning and implementing large-scale projects with limited or no reference to community groups. I use 'social planning' to describe all this 'other' work. However, 'inter-agency work' and more recently 'programme bending' (of which more later) are terms which are sometimes used to describe it.

The idea that community workers work with 'the community' in a neutral way on issues determined by that community is, to say the least, open to debate. We are all bound to seek out persons in the community with whom we believe we can work and who want to undertake the activities which we think are the most valuable. Neither, on the whole, do communities choose us to work for

79

them: we choose the community. Thus, all community work includes elements of social planning, since the worker or agency plays a large part in deciding where the worker should work and what activities he or she should become involved with.

There are three main types of activity which constitute a social planning approach within community work: doing work *for* groups (as opposed to acting as a facilitator); acting as an *advocate or mediator* with other organisations on an existing group's behalf; and *direct* work: setting up projects or working with service providers and policy makers without reference to a community group. However, only the last of these could properly be called social planning; the first two are, perhaps, stages towards it, since the worker is no longer acting primarily as an enabler.

Doing work *for* groups

Undertaking activities *for* community groups can include carrying out any of the tasks which the members might otherwise be expected to do, and even on occasion acting as chair, secretary or treasurer. Sensitively carried out, undertaking activities *for* groups in this way can strengthen the confidence, capacities and autonomy of group members. However, if it is done without due thought it can have the effect of making people dependent. There are also many times when a group would collapse unless the worker fulfilled such roles. Ideally, however, doing work *for* groups should only be undertaken for a limited time and preferably on the understanding that group members should take over that work at a later date.

Acting as an *advocate* for a group

I once helped the secretary of an organisation for disabled people get the installation of a telephone paid for by the social services department after the organisation's application had been refused. The case had not been presented well and inappropriate legislation had been cited. The application was only granted when I wrote to the department citing the appropriate legislation. In theory, I could have helped the secretary write another letter appealing against the decision, but that might have taken some time, besides which the secretary had rather given up the struggle and might not have wished to write another letter. It was also important to get the decision reversed quickly.

Similarly, a colleague of mine working in a local authority helped an organisation obtain its annual grant after its original application had been refused by the City Council. Again, the initial application had been badly presented by the group. Normally the worker would have been present at the relevant local authority committee to speak for the organisation. However, he was ill and certain officials opposed to the organisation presented the application in an unfavourable light. Luckily he was able to bring the matter up at the next committee and got the decision reversed. There are several reasons why the worker could not work with the secretary of this organisation to ensure that the original application was well presented. First, he might not have been invited to help. Second, the secretary might have resented his 'interference' if he had offered help. Third, he could have been wrong; the application might have elicited the grant. Fourth, he was probably busy servicing several different groups and might not have had the time to do the necessary work with the secretary of the group to ensure a successful application. Finally, ensuring the organisation got its grant probably also required the use of contacts which only he had, by virtue of his position in the local authority.

At a more general level, Leo Smith's work is a good example of advocacy in practice. As 'Participation Officer' for a London borough, his job was to ensure that community groups had access to the local authority, and he spent a good deal of time working within the authority to ensure that appropriate access policies were initiated (Leo Smith, 1981).

Another aspect of the advocacy role is that of the broker between, say, a community group and a local authority. The two parties may often take issue over a matter because they see it from different points of view and cannot appreciate the perspective of the other. They then find themselves in fixed positions and do not listen to what the other has to say. The worker can sometimes help by explaining the perception of one party to the other, identifying clearly the point at issue and ultimately bringing the parties together to resolve it. However, a lot of preparatory work usually needs to be done before the parties are brought together, and it can only work if they both want it. Goetschius (1969, pp. 93–5) has a useful section on the steps to take when acting in this way.

Acting as advocate or broker has many dangers. The danger of making groups dependent on the worker is ever present: it is so often quicker for workers to do the job themselves, and the resulting outcome is so obviously to the immediate benefit of the group, that 'product' seems more important than process. Yet the uniqueness of community development work is that members of the community learn to do things for themselves.

A related danger is that the worker becomes a buffer between the community group and the target organisation. I think I acted in this way during the incident mentioned in Chapter 3 when I explained to the members of a group that it was no use seeking permission to use a football pitch on a Sunday because local authority policy forbade this. When its members did not accept what I said, I found myself trying to 'persuade' them! I was, in effect, acting as an apologist for the target organisation and protecting public officials from having to explain and justify their policies to the community.

Community workers can also sometimes become quite pessimistic about the possibilities of change and may overestimate the difficulties. Often a great deal can be achieved when the group members are enthusiastic and apply political pressure themselves.

Ideally, advocacy on behalf of a community group by a worker should only be undertaken with the knowledge and consent of the group. An aim should also be to try to ensure that the group learns to act as its own advocate. However, community workers who are in contact with a range of officials and politicians have many opportunities to influence the political and administrative process to the advantage of the communities with which they work – by ensuring that details of new funding arrangements are widely circulated, or speaking in favour of a group at a particular meeting, for example – and it would be foolish not to take such opportunities.

Direct work: setting up projects or working with service providers and policy makers

A director of social services once said to me, 'It's useful to have people like you employed without a particular service responsibility because you have the time to look at needs on the ground and find new ways of meeting them'. That is how community workers spend much of their time. They set up law centres, youth employment schemes, women's refuges, to name but a few. However, this role requires a range of specific skills. First, we have to analyse needs and identify how these can be met. Second, we need the interactional and organisational skills necessary to bring people together and to motivate them to work on problems and find and implement solutions. Third, we need the skills of fundraising, project planning and management.

The social planning role in community work applies most directly when the work undertaken by the worker has no direct and immediate link with a community group. For instance, if a community group goes out of existence, you may decide to continue working on the issues which the group was taking up, but under the auspices of your own agency or with a group of professionals.

A tenants' association, which I had helped establish, collapsed. It had been concerned with the modernisation of council houses, and I thought it important that the work it was doing should be continued. So I carried out a survey of the tenants' satisfaction with the houses which had already been modernised and fed back the results to the housing department in order to seek to influence policy.

On other occasions, an opportunity to provide a necessary service may arise when a community group does not exist, and it may not be appropriate to try to bring one into existence. There were a number of very large families in the neighbourhood and I thought that a locally based Family Planning Association (FPA) clinic might serve the needs of the local people better than the city-centre one. So, liaising with the FPA, local GPs and health visitors, I arranged for family planning advice to be provided one day per week at the existing well-baby clinic.

If I had wanted to take a community development approach to this problem, I could have spoken with local people to see if they agreed that there was a need, and were interested in trying to get such a clinic. This process would almost certainly have been a longer one and may not have worked, since, when a worker starts with an issue or activity which interests *him* or *her*, it does not always prove possible to ensure that an autonomous community group forms to take it up.

I once discussed tenant management of council housing with a local authority councillor. I suggested that recent legislation made it

possible for council tenants to turn their estates into housing co-
operatives. His reply was 'We'll give the estates over to tenants to
form co-operatives any time they want. But what they want is a
good service and not to be bothered with running their estates
themselves.'

In general terms I think he is right. I primarily want to enjoy
myself in my spare time and not to do more work. But I also think
that if consumers are not involved in some major way in influencing
services, those services deteriorate. Therefore, as people are sometimes not able or prepared to participate in influencing those services,
it makes sense for community workers themselves, in some situations
at least, to work with other professionals to improve them.

By virtue of our ability to build organisations, our ability to help
others build organisations, our ability to communicate and our
personal knowledge of and contact with the people of the community we serve, community workers are in a good position to influence service development. Legislative changes, the frequent though
often short-lived availability of funds for specific purposes, and new
fashions in social policy all require 'social entrepreneurs' (read
'community workers') who can work with others to create appropriate organisations and initiatives and who are concerned to meet
the real needs of excluded people.

The case for taking a social planning approach is based on the
reality that: helping community groups obtain real power is extraordinarily problematic, difficult and slow; the disadvantaged people
with and for whom we work want better services *now*; and finally,
our own meal tickets are mostly provided by a state which, at least
ostensibly, wants us to develop services for high need groups. It is,
thus, legitimate for community workers to use pretty much the same
skills which we use in the community development process to work
with other professionals to provide better services for high-need
groups.

One way to start this collaborative process is for community
workers to structure liaison with other professionals into their
work plan. When good contacts are made, better ways are eventually found of delivering services.

Establishing good contacts with other professionals requires,
first, an ability to 'see the world from their eyes', and second, a
concern to assist them with their own work, if possible. If one is
genuinely interested in how 'the other' sees the world, it is not

usually difficult to establish good relationships. However, different professionals usually all see a situation slightly differently. This is because their starting points are different. That is one of the reasons why professionals from different agencies often have difficulty working together. It is also important for each worker in, say, an inter-agency liaison group to explain the 'mission' of their own organisation initially and to explain how they see the issue in question. Then each agency has an opportunity to understand how the others perceive the situation. Otherwise, the group is likely to get bogged down with people talking at cross purposes due to conflicting but unstated assumptions about goals and means.

Corina (1977) concluded that contact with middle rank officers was one of the most effective ways of obtaining influence on local authorities. Other evidence is provided by Levin (1981) who describes the process by which a local authority took a decision to build a major housing scheme. There was no point at which a firm decision to go ahead with the project was made; the authority gradually became committed to it. Only by being involved on a continuing basis would it have been possible to affect the course of events. Community workers, especially those working in governmental organisations, are often in an excellent position to influence such processes.

Some examples of a social planning approach in practice

'Bottom up' work cannot be effective unless large institutions, such as local authority departments, are receptive to community need and are prepared to co-ordinate their own activities in order to respond effectively to expressed needs from the community. My former colleague, Judith Bevan, who ran a community project in Wales, met bi-monthly with the deputy heads of the local authority departments (together) to ensure that this co-ordination happened. Similarly, when establishing a comprehensive renewal strategy for the upper Rhymney Valley, Caerphilly County Borough Council first put into place an interdepartmental co-ordinating mechanism.

Service strategies and influence strategies in social planning

Some 'social planning' initiatives consist of pressure group (influence) work where the driving force is professional workers, some of whom are perhaps working in a personal capacity while others are working in their professional capacity (although the latter is rare in Britain today). A campaign to stop cuts in a service would be an example.

Other social planning approaches are, primarily, service strategies where a worker, an organisation, an agency (or several of these) seeks to obtain resources to develop a new initiative..

Many agencies are involved both in service strategies and influence strategies. For instance, Age Concern groups in Britain set up projects such as hospital discharge schemes, but they also attempt to influence governmental policy with regard to the needs of older people (in addition to any 'bottom up' community development work they do).

Usually, campaigning organisations are not successful in obtaining public or charitable funds to employ personnel to run campaigns. Thus, the majority of projects set up by means of a social planning approach are service projects, and some of these obtain resources to employ staff. For example, a group of professionals from a range of agencies which was originally campaigning for better provision for homeless people might eventually obtain resources to establish accommodation for such people and create a new service agency. In such cases the community worker who was a member of the group or was servicing it would be involved in designing and possibly managing the new service.

In today's world, many important issues bridge several service areas. Play, for example, relates to recreation departments, education departments and social services departments. Therefore, workers who are trying to effect a change will often need to spend time as members of inter-departmental or inter-professional groups. These bodies may be temporary, such as, working parties, or more formal semi permanent organisations. Sometimes no formal body will exist but the worker will be liaising with a range of organisations in order to facilitate a policy change, for example.

The 'professional' neighbourhood organisation

A powerful force on the estate where I once worked was an umbrella organisation consisting of professionals. It had initially been established by the vicar with the purpose of examining needs in the locality, but it later included representatives of community groups. I became a member but also acted as its 'chief executive' in that I carried out what it decided should be done – for instance, organising a newsletter. Similarly, a community worker on a council estate in Cardiff set up an action group of professionals, with sub-committees on particular subject areas, which designed and implemented different schemes. Corina (1977, pp. 74–8) gives an interesting example of area councillor committees which consisted of councillors, officers and residents, and which were able to discuss policy matters *before* the council took firm decisions. Newcastle's Priority Area Teams are another example.

When forming an organisation for professionals at neighbourhood level, there may be the usual problems of inertia, apathy even, yet it is often easy to set up an initial meeting. However, in order for a group of professionals to stay in existence, an activity is needed which they can all work on. But they will each have their special interests. Therefore, if the group decides to undertake a project to benefit older people, schoolteachers are unlikely to be interested, for example. The answer is to find a project or series of projects which fire the interest of a reasonable number of them.

Also, groups of professionals can easily fail to encourage community involvement, and I would be concerned about such a group which did not try to create this in some way.

Specialist community work and social planning

In 'generic' neighbourhood community development work, there is some danger that the worker will not use a social planning approach enough. However, the danger for most specialist community workers, especially those working in statutory agencies, is that they will not engage in community development (bottom-up) work at all. This is because, increasingly, statutory agencies are employing staff to develop services *for* high-need groups.

In such work the starting point is what the service agency wants. However, a new service to a disadvantaged community will probably not work well unless the consumers are involved in deciding what it should be and providing feedback as it is implemented. And they will not easily become involved if it is a 'top-down' service with a minimal amount of consumer consultation, which is what specialist community work is usually expected by service providers to offer. This creates difficulties for the worker because it often proves impossible to involve the consumers effectively on such a basis.

Specialist community workers employed by non-statutory agencies, such as Women's Aid, Shelter, housing associations, common ownership development agencies, community relations councils, Mind, Mencap, Age Concern and the like, often have a reasonable amount of freedom, in principle, to use community development as well as social planning approaches. However, most of these agencies are funded by government to provide services, and they only receive their annual grant on this basis. Also, their staff may operate over too wide an area for any in-depth community development work to be undertaken.

As a generic neighbourhood-based community worker, one can walk the streets, get into contact with local people and start the community development process. Differences of social class, housing tenure, educational attainment, occupation, culture and residence will usually separate workers fairly distinctly from the neighbourhood community in which they work. Thus, it is easy for workers to know when they are working with other professionals or councillors rather than the local people or vice versa. The corresponding community development approach with a community of interest or need is to get into contact with people either through their representatives (for example, the parents of children with learning difficulties) or through the people who work with them: doctors, teachers, social workers, and so on. However, when promoting self-help groups, of which a prime purpose is to provide mutual support for people sharing a particular need, it is often the case that 'professionals' are also members of the group because they share the same condition. For instance, a community worker once worked with a support group for cancer sufferers. While one of the leaders was a health visitor who was primarily there in a professional capacity, she also had cancer. Roles may not be very clear-cut in work with communities of need.

When a specialist community worker sets up an instrumental group as opposed to an expressive (self-help) group (as in the above example), it often becomes even more difficult to distinguish between consumers and professionals. A county-wide organisation was established by a community worker working for a social services department, the purpose of which was to take various actions to improve housing and work opportunities for people with learning difficulties. The majority of the committee consisted of parents. (Let us consider parents as consumers, although they are primarily the representatives of the consumers). Several of those parents had been active volunteers with Mencap for years, and in many cases were more 'professional' than the social services staff. One of them was now also employed by Mencap. Another worked part-time in an Adult Training Centre. Other members of the committee (parents) included a bank manager and representatives from the health authority. In this particular group there were no individuals with a learning difficulty. The two social services department community workers specialising in work with people with learning difficulties were also full members of the group. But one of them had a child with learning difficulties. Thus, this organisation contained both consumers and professionals some of whom were there in several capacities.

In work with communities of interest/need the important distinction between the facilitator and the community group which they are servicing often also becomes blurred. For instance, the establishment of a voluntary Age Concern group in a small town may have been fostered by a paid community worker. The group might then go on to acquire its own resources in order to employ a worker. This worker would probably act not only as the general secretary of the organisation, running the services it provided, but also as a specialist community development worker helping other groups concerned with the needs of older people to emerge at a more local level. Thus, an increasing number of organisations now exist which have paid staff and which are both service agencies and community development agencies at the same time.

The roles which professional community workers are called upon to play in such groups can be conflicting and confusing. On the one hand, you may have brought people together to form the organisation by using your 'enabling' skills. On the other hand, you may also play a major organisational role and be, in effect, the secretary or chair of the group.

In such a group the worker might, in addition, share the same circumstances or condition as the 'ordinary' group members (for example, be from an ethnic minority or be a single parent). On this point, it is noticeable that the motivation of many professional workers is, in many cases, related to personal experience, of oppression, bereavement, or some other difficult personal circumstance.

The roles of enabler and organiser (or leader) are difficult to combine. In the organisation mentioned above, which was concerned with providing accommodation for people with learning difficulties, the social services department (SSD) provided funding and other resources which were not always adequate. The unfortunate community workers probably shared the criticisms which the group members had of the SSD and, yet, they were also the spokespersons for that organisation, which they could not criticise openly. Clear thinking, careful planning and excellent communication skills are necessary to handle the problems which arise in such situations.

It is also a mistake to think that professionals necessarily know how to operate in groups and organisations. They generally need to learn how to do this well just as the members of community groups need to do.

From social planning to community development?

As we saw earlier many employers of community workers today, especially those in the statutory sector, are more concerned with improved service provision than with community development. For instance, a housing department I know well employs tenant liaison officers primarily to feed back views to the local authority which will help it improve its housing policy. While such work is not community development, it may provide a way into community development. Thus, the way into 'bottom up' work for many professional workers may be through initiatives which are initially of a social planning kind. A 'Take Care' project, run by the Wales Council for Voluntary Action, aimed to repair the homes of poor elderly owner-occupiers using unemployed local people. However, the staff running the scheme also set up a number of community groups consisting, in the main, of older people in order to oversee the scheme in each locality. This mechanism allowed local elderly people to meet to discuss their needs and to raise these with service providers. This is an example of one of the ways in which community workers operating as social planners can bring a community development focus to their work. If you are employed in a social planning role, figure out ways of doing community development work too.

Dilemmas of social planning

The danger of community development workers moving into social planning is that they are to some degree forsaking one of the first principles of community work, namely, 'starting where people are at'. They run the risk of merely getting done what they want to see done, ignoring what members of the community want and failing to involve them in the process. They may also find that co-ordinating and managing the projects they set up takes all their time and prevents them from giving much attention to 'community-centred' activities which may not be so productive in terms of concrete achievements. Therefore, when we initiate schemes without reference in the first instance to a community group, we must ensure that we still spend time on 'community-centred' activity and seek to involve members of the community whenever appropriate.

Another reason for adopting a social planning approach is that there are so many needs which require meeting and so few members of the community who are prepared and able to meet them that it is unrealistic to expect those people to take up everything. A community worker in the USA was helping residents of what in Britain we would call a caravan site to buy their homes collectively and set up a management co-op. The residents seemed reluctant to see the process through until the worker told them they could employ somebody to collect rents, undertake repairs, and so on. They had, quite understandably, balked at the implication that they would have to undertake all the work on an unpaid basis. If we have assessed needs correctly, and if we set up the project properly, there is likely to be considerable community support for schemes which we initiate in a 'social planning' way.

It also needs to be remembered that there is a 'community work' way and a 'non-community work' way of going about meeting needs. A worker identified a need for youth provision and set up a youth club one evening per week. It went well, so he opened two, three, four, five nights per week. Then he found he had become a youth worker! A true community worker would approach the problem in a different way. Perhaps they would start a club one evening per week to reveal the need and show what could be done. But they would spend the rest of their time trying to involve others, church organisations, residents, or the district youth officer, for example, in creating a mechanism whereby others would take responsibility at a certain point so that the worker could withdraw and move on to something else.

Getting others to take responsibility for a project is often difficult, however. For instance, we may argue the case with potential funders for resources, but with no success. Ultimately we may decide to run the project, perhaps in our spare time, to show that it works. Then, when the project is running, our own agency or possibly another agency may take an interest and adopt it as a matter of policy. However, many agencies will allow us to develop our own special interest, but will let it die when we leave. If we want it to continue, we must also work to structure the change we have initiated into the agency or other agencies. A basic principle to follow is that, if we want to implement a change which will involve another party, we must make sure we involve that party and help it develop a sense of ownership at an early stage of the planning process. Thus, they will have done the thinking with us and will not feel they are being presented with an 'all or nothing' decision later on, which can stiffen resistance.

The case against social planning

The legitimation of the community development worker comes from being in frequent contact with members of the community and from helping at least some of them organise to get the community's needs met. This process is based on the idea that people learn best how to do things by trial and error. If you get involved in direct service provision, this means, at best, that you are not spending time on community development work. At worst, the community worker or project can be destructive, since some of the services which community workers are engaged to promote are misconceived, under-resourced and generally disempower communities.

The project planning process

The main concern of service professionals is not at the planning level. However, in order to ensure that the health visitor, or teacher, for instance, 'at the sharp end' does his or her job properly, planning and managerial tasks have to be undertaken. If they are undertaken badly, both consumers and field staff suffer. In project planning and management, one's mental set has to switch from the relatively mono-dimensional focus of the service professional to the multi-dimensional focus of the planner who has to take many different requirements into account at the same time. Whether one is establishing a one-evening-a-week advice service staffed by volunteers or a complex scheme employing hundreds of staff, it is necessary to consider the following points.

Who wants it?

This point is well made by Smiley (1982). He recounts how every member of his family thought the others wanted to take a trip to Abilene, though did not want to go themselves. However, they only discovered this after a disastrous day out. Setting up projects which nobody wants is easily done. Somebody suggests 'Let's run a carnival' expecting that is what the others in the group want. They do not, but say yes because they think he wants it and will make sure it works. It is always useful to try to work out who wants a particular project and why. Often, nobody wants it!

What need will it meet?

If the proposal is, for instance, to run a newsletter, what is hoped that this will achieve? What will be different from the present situation if the newsletter is established? People often focus on the means rather than on the end. We need to think about ends.

What alternatives are there?

Once there is clarity about the need which is to be met, alternative ways of meeting it should be evaluated. If there are high numbers of isolated elderly people in an area, what are alternative ways of reducing their isolation? The point of evaluating alternatives is so that we do not spring into action to run a project in a particular way without thinking about the most effective way of meeting the need.

Who else has tried this and what were the problems?

We often go into a particular project because we want it to succeed rather than because there is a likelihood of success. These pitfalls can sometimes be avoided if we discover from other people or from books how such a project can be run, rather than re-inventing the often-broken wheel. A related point is:

Will it succeed?

As we wish, presumably, to be involved with successful projects it makes sense to estimate the chances of success. This does not mean that we should only seek to establish projects which are bound to succeed but that most of our projects should have a better than even chance of success.

What resources are required?

Resources include money, equipment, people and time. Where are these resources available? Are they adequate? Can they be obtained in time? Resources are often too few, and there is a danger that we will cut our coat too skimpily. In my experience, it is usually better to employ one worker on a good salary with adequate backup than to try to squeeze two under-resourced workers out of the money available, who will soon leave for a better job if they are any good. Similarly, it is best not to appoint staff about whom one has major doubts because nobody else is available. It is better to re-advertise. Also, most projects take longer to get going than we think. Try to plan the time it will take accurately (then double it!).

Where is the engine?

At least one person has to be determined to make a project work, to be the 'engine', who will burn the midnight oil if necessary. If there is no other engine, the community worker may need to become the engine and hope, perhaps in vain, that a leader (or leaders) emerge as the project gets going.

Obstacles

Does the project run counter to a major existing policy? Are those whose co-operation is needed too busy, or apathetic? Do certain powerful people have a vested interest in its failure? If so, how can they be converted or bypassed? Resnick and Patti (1980) make some excellent points about the importance of predicting resistance in organisational change and preparing one's response to that resistance. (See also, Brager and Holloway, 1978). The best prepared community workers are those who familiarise themselves as much as possible with the internal politics both of their own organisation and of likely target organisations *in advance* of any project, since they will then have a good eye for spotting both opportunities and potential problems.

A further obstacle can be lack of agency expertise. There is always a slow learning curve for any organisation which starts a new activity; to run a complex project in a field where the agency has no existing expertise is usually disastrous.

Who else should be consulted or involved?

The times when potential supporters can be turned into opponents because we have failed to inform, consult or involve them early are without number. In our keenness to get moving we may forget to ask ourselves who else could appropriately be involved. There may also be persons whom we do not wish to involve, and ways need to be found of excluding them as neatly as possible.

The need for allies

It is usually more difficult to get things done than to do nothing. So any new project needs allies. But allies need to be in place well before the project starts, which again underlines the importance of permanent contact-making. Allies may sometimes provide inside information which helps our case. Sometimes, however, that information is secret and we cannot use it freely without compromising our ally. Much forethought is necessary in these kinds of situations.

What kind of organisational structure is necessary?

Most new non-statutory projects need constitutions. They may need to register as a charity or a limited-liability company. Questions such as the composition and size of the management committee will need to be considered, and there are often two conflicting needs here. Effective decisions are best taken by groups of fewer than ten. But a small group often has to have legitimacy through a wider constituency, which usually means occasional meetings of a large group which, in theory, sets policy. In reality, however, a large group cannot even set policy easily. Its ability to do so depends on how far the small 'executive' group prepares the decisions for the policy-making group to decide about.

Another dilemma is whether to have constituent organisations send representatives to the management committee, in which case there is likely to be some dead wood, or to seek out committed and able individuals. A related point is how to be representative in a real rather than a tokenistic way (for instance, the all-male white group which then co-opts a token woman or black person). In principle, the way round this is to consider *at the beginning* all the interests which should be represented and to ensure that the invited membership reflects as far as possible the kinds of diversity necessary.

There is a perennial tension between the need for both participation and decisive action, to which there are no easy solutions. See Holloway and Otto (1985), for useful tips about organisation, and Forbes, (1998), for assistance on constitutional and legal points.

'No' can be a very good answer

After doing careful pre-planning, most of us feel reluctant not to go ahead, even if it looks a high-risk project. However, failure at a later stage would be even worse. So it is no disgrace to pull out if feasibility work shows the project is not likely to be viable.

Worker role in social planning approaches

In getting new projects or services off the ground workers have to decide whether to play the role of facilitator and withdraw as soon as they can or whether to play an organising and, later, a managerial role, with the concomitant danger that they will not be able to find somebody else to hand the work over to.

Project implementation

The implementation stage is the time we actually get the resources, set up the organisation, design a work plan, rent the building, hire and induct staff and do the work. Of these, hiring staff is perhaps the most important. Working out a systematic procedure for ensuring that as far as possible the person who is best for the job gets it pays enormous dividends. Hiring staff is often done without due care. Many organisations have equal opportunity recruitment procedures, which can be useful here. It pays to learn about such procedures.

One problem encountered when hiring staff for community projects is that local people often want to hire somebody from the neighbourhood, not recognising either that this could infringe the law or that, as it is often difficult to hire good staff, it is usually best to cast the net as widely as possible. There is no simple answer to this one, but be prepared for it to come up, and try to work out in advance how best to handle it.

We can be certain about one thing in the implementation phase: it will throw up unforeseen problems! Therefore, the new venture has to be carefully watched at this stage so that these problems can be sorted out. That is, good feedback mechanisms have to be put into place which will reveal potential problems quickly, so they can be corrected before they become serious.

Project management

The purpose of this section is not to cover project management in depth, but to give a few pointers to community workers who find themselves in managerial positions.

The need for an overview

Fieldworkers are usually effective advocates for the work on the ground which they are engaged to do. However, they may not easily see that, on occasion, the needs of another project may have to take precedence or that a particular line of approach which they favour might jeopardise future funding. Or they may all wish to innovate in different directions at once. Managers, on the other hand, need to ensure that agencies develop their work consistently in a particular direction and to take a wide and long view, 'keeping their fingers on all the ends'.

Agency/project maintenance

A project does not automatically run for ever. It may be necessary to re-negotiate resources each year, and that may mean adapting the project slightly to obtain different kinds of funding. Or there may be changes in, say, the political make-up of the council, which means that the funders need re-convincing that the project has value. You need to ensure too that the structure of the organisation remains appropriate to the tasks in hand. A voluntary management committee, for example, needs infusions of new blood from time to time and has to find ways of keeping in touch with the staff.

Agency maintenance ranges from raising the necessary funding to attending the mayor's banquet, and from making sure the staff get their pay cheques on time (some voluntary organisations are very sloppy about this) to ensuring the central heating is working properly! Innovatory agencies usually run on a shoestring and operate from inadequate buildings. Managers have to ensure, in particular, that the conditions of employment are reasonably adequate. While they do not have to undertake all the above mentioned tasks themselves – though in an emergency they may have to sweep flood water from the basement, for instance – they need to ensure a system is in place whereby all this gets done.

Many agency staff are excellent fieldworkers but fail to convince important outsiders that they are doing a good job. Yet, effective public relations is vitally important. In statutory agencies, it largely means ensuring that those in the higher echelons of the organisation know about and appreciate the value of the particular service which is being delivered. In non-statutory organisations, the emphasis needs to be on showing the wider public, politicians and potential funders the value of the work through well-produced reports, press releases, open days, talks to other organisations, and the like. In particular it means trying to ensure those whose support you need 'walk the streets with you' because that is how that they will come to appreciate the reality of what you do.

A sense of strategy

When I was a university lecturer, I once spent a good deal of time involved in local projects. I later thought that it would be a more appropriate use of my time to develop short courses for practitioners, which I did. Such strategic decisions need primarily to be made at the agency level, which obviously requires consultation. But, once the strategy has been decided, it is often the manager who has to ensure that the strategy is adhered to. However, a strategy to concentrate on one area, by definition, means that other areas must be neglected.

Financial planning and work planning

Many agencies do not plan their work effectively. All workers and agencies need a realistic monthly (or perhaps bi-monthly or quarterly) plan of work. There should also be a budget, and a running check should be kept on expenditure on a monthly basis, as well as on whether planned objectives have been achieved.

Similarly, the sequence of actions in a project needs to be properly worked out. In the case of conferences, for instance, the venue needs to be booked before publicity material is issued. Enough advance notice also needs to be given for delegates to apply to their agencies for funding. These and similar points need to be taken account of when setting the date: otherwise time can run out. This kind of approach is sometimes called 'critical path analysis'.

Day-to-day work also needs to be planned properly. How many staff meetings have you gone to where no record is kept of decisions, or somebody has come with a poorly thought-out idea which has been discussed for an hour before people realise the matter has to be deferred to the next meeting so that more work can be done on it? In how many organisations does the chair not know what he or she is supposed to be doing? Similarly, how often have you taken part in a meeting without being clear why, and what you want? When we are pressed, even thirty seconds' thought about our objectives in advance of the meeting can help.

Community workers also often find themselves on management committees, the main purpose of which is to set policy, hire and manage senior staff and evaluate outcomes. Yet we are often not very knowledgeable about these managerial responsibilities. Therefore, it is important for community workers to learn about management, preferably prior to becoming a manager.

People management

The greater the sense of ownership which the staff (including volunteers) in an organisation develop, the greater the commitment they will have and the more effective their work will be. Closely related to this is the vital need we all have to be recognised.

A major task of a manager is to resource his or her staff. Part of this is ensuring that they work in reasonable conditions. Another part is being available when they want advice. A lot of it is valuing them and their work, giving them the space to take risks, knowing when to offer help, being concerned about their long-term development, even when this will take them out of the agency, utilising their talents, and listening to their ideas. There is also the question of teamwork, and a manager of a community project would be well advised to take a short course in team building.

For many community workers, resourcing people is the only side of staff management which is valued. There is, however, another dimension, which I call 'quality control'.

A senior community worker was resourcing several less experienced workers. However, the reports which one of them was providing about his work seemed a bit odd. So she checked up, to find that he had been fabricating his records! There are many more examples of poor practice. Some of us are slow at writing reports. Some of us regularly manage to annoy our colleagues. Yet others fail to plan with sufficient attention to detail. It is ultimately the responsibility of the manager to ensure that the service to the consumer is as effective as possible, which means combining the resourcing role with the quality control role.

It is sometimes difficult to work out if a community worker is effective or not, because you cannot easily see what they are doing. Therefore, managers need to put systems in place which help them get the best possible 'handle' on their staff's work.

Many people in community work want to be liked and do not find the quality control aspects of management easy. One common mistake is for the team leader to give the impression that the team members are all equal when he or she is, ultimately, the boss. It is important, in my view, that such points are made clear at the beginning of a project rather than when a crisis occurs. The existence of an agreed and written work plan coupled with review meetings assists a manager to raise difficult issues with staff who are not performing.

It is quite difficult to value and respect staff who are difficult, lazy or not very competent and not prepared to work at it. I think the trick is valuing the *person* and complimenting them on what they do well, while not accepting poor work, explaining why and ensuring a programme is put into place to assist the worker to improve. (I did not say it was easy, though!)

Several years ago Peters and Waterman (1982) and Peters and Austin (1985) undertook some research into what makes for successful organisations. Their main conclusions, still relevant today, were:

- valuing staff;
- being passionately concerned that the customers (consumers) are satisfied and that staff adhere to central values, such as, the vital importance of good customer service;
- constant innovation and entrepreneurship;
- good leadership and
- 'management by wandering about' (that is, by ensuring that there is considerable informal face-to-face contact between managers and staff).

While these attributes emerged from studies of successful companies, they apply equally well to all effective organisations.

On occasion, the team leader will have to take unpopular decisions or direct reluctant staff to do or not do certain things. When managers take such decisions, they should try to consult widely before taking them. Remember, too, that people in authority often do not realise how easy it is to abuse this power. A chance remark or a mild criticism can seriously undermine more junior staff, for example. Also, if possible *write down* compliments to staff, but *say* critical things. The written word leaves a permanent record.

Managing volunteers

In this section I am referring to voluntary work in the most usual sense of the word, where the volunteers work under the auspices of an agency. My frame of reference now is also neighbourhood community work where the volunteers may be from outside the locality and may also be of a different class and culture from residents.

Some community groups require services which neither the worker nor other members of the community are able to provide. For instance, many members of the disabled club with which I worked required help with shopping and transport. There may also be projects which a worker wishes to initiate, such as a youth club, which no local people seem able or willing to take on. If it is done sensitively, volunteers from another locality and of a different social class can be successfully involved in many community activities.

If volunteers are needed for complex and responsible tasks, it is necessary to spend a good deal of time helping them to think through the implications of the work: the stress it may place on them, for example. For some activities it is important to take up references, make thorough enquiries and sometimes undertake legal checks about their suitability.

Unless you spend a considerable amount of time with volunteers before they start work, during which you will also be assessing which kind of activity would be most suitable for them, you may wish to give them simple tasks first, such as delivering a newsletter, after which they can be moved on to more difficult tasks. We must be careful here though. As many volunteers leave because they are underused as those that leave because they are overworked. We also need to consider how to provide continuing support, through a regular group, perhaps. Volunteers, too, need to understand that if their work is to be of value they need to attend reliably. They also have needs, for out-of-pocket expenses and training, for instance. In short, they need a contract and to be managed, rather like paid staff.

In Britain the National Centre for Volunteering can provide many helpful leaflets on this subject.

A few really good volunteers eventually become colleagues who develop and manage their own area of interest without a great deal of supervision or support.

Local activists as paid community workers?

Many projects employ local people, often on a part-time basis, and this is one of the strengths of community work. There are dangers however. Grace, a local resident, carried out a great deal of advice work in her own home. When she had been associated with our project for about five years, we began paying her to run two sessions in our advice centre. These sessions gradually increased, and, after another three years, we employed her full-time. This was the length of time she needed in order to build up her confidence and become accustomed to the ethos and many unwritten customs of a professional agency.

Jack, the leader of the adventure playground had a local voluntary helper, Greg. When money became available for a second playleader, Greg applied and Jack did not discourage him. But Greg was not liked by the children and there was no way the committee could have appointed him. When he did not get the job, he caused a great disturbance for some weeks, physically assaulting Jack, who had to close the playground for a time and ban Greg from it. It is difficult to say what Jack should have told Greg when he wanted to apply for the job. Perhaps somebody from the committee should have pointed out to Greg that there would be other candidates too and there was no guarantee he would get the job. Well-worked-out hiring procedures, which should also have been explained to Greg, would have helped.

When local activists become employed as community workers they bring a great deal to the work. But because they live in the locality they may have a rather subjective view of the situation. They may also have local enemies. Community activists may be excellent voluntary workers, but as unpaid workers they could play to their strengths. Professionals sometimes have to work on projects which they find uncongenial.

If community activists are to be employed as community workers, they may need substantial help to become enablers rather than leaders and to develop relevant analytical interactional and report-writing skills. This jump is not always easy to make. It takes time, training and continuing support. While community development work consists of transferring skills and confidence to other people, the business of transferring these skills is a high skill in itself. We are not doing anybody any favours if we pretend that these 'facilitating' skills are 'common currency' and if we employ people who cannot do the job.

Local management?

Some community workers consider that to be employed by a community group is the ideal, since one is accountable directly to the people with whom one is working. However, community groups tend to be short-lived, have difficulty in managing money, do not always take decisions well, may have a conservative leadership which is easily threatened and, thus, lack the ability to manage a professional worker. If you are employed by a community group you may get no guidance and you may have to support the group rather than get support from it. You may not get paid regularly and may have to work out your own salary and national insurance contributions. A community group may also become over-directive, particularly if the work experience of the members is in employment which has an authoritarian style of management. You may not be allowed to work with organisations in the locality with which your employers are not in sympathy. Finally, community groups often have quite enough to do without having to manage staff. Think carefully before you arrange for a small local group to manage a worker.

Supervising professional community workers

In order to resource professional community workers effectively, to enable them to develop their skills and to ensure that they work on their areas of weakness, regular supervision is necessary. If two workers are working on the same project they can sometimes learn a great deal by undertaking it together. Nevertheless, supervision is essentially individual. Effective community workers plan their work in advance, agree those plans with their supervisor, monitor and evaluate how far it has been possible to achieve planned objectives and modify the plan accordingly. In order for a worker to be accountable to an agency, these plans and the outcomes arising from their implementation have to be written down as retrievable records. But it is difficult to plan and evaluate on one's own. Inexperienced workers, especially, require experienced supervisors who can provide 'critical support', and staff need to know that they are going to be held accountable. Thus, meetings with the supervisor will usually cover the work undertaken in the previous month or so and, at least, a verbal evaluation of it; plans for future work; and any problems the worker may be facing. With new employees, students on placement and at times of staff reviews, the emphasis needs to be on what the worker has learned, what they think they do well and less well, what new areas of knowledge and skill they think they need to gain and how these objectives can be reached. Supervision also needs to include an opportunity for the worker to comment on the support offered by the supervisor and the agency.

The personal dimension to supervision can be difficult because it relates to individual qualities such as perseverance, tolerance, and so on. Supervisors are, in my view, not doing their job properly if they studiously avoid the 'personal'. On the other hand, they have to be careful not to overstep the boundary between that part of the personal which relates to professional effectiveness and the entirely private concerns of the member of staff. I usually ask the person I am supervising to determine the agenda. This gives them the space to raise issues which are of concern to them and often gives me an opportunity, later, to add my own view.

All staff need to know that the organisation has expectations about the quality of work and that, if this is unsatisfactory, steps will be taken to ensure that a worker performs appropriately, or, eventually, leaves. Thus, hiring, disciplining and, ultimately, firing policies are necessary. If a worker has been getting appropriate supervision but their work is still unsatisfactory, steps need to be taken in accordance with this policy. However, the first step has to be to point out exactly what is not adequate, to indicate what an adequate performance would consist of and how it would be measured, and to try to get the worker to agree both to this and to the steps to take which will improve his or her performance. It is also important, if a worker is not performing well, to indicate this early at supervision sessions rather than to convey it as a bombshell at an annual review.

Working the system

Specht (1975) identified four broad 'modes of intervention' in relation to promoting social change: collaboration, campaign, contest and violence. (We look at campaigns and contest in Chapter 7.)

A collaborative approach (which can also be called working the system) is applicable when there is consensus about the issue between, let us say, the community and the local authority. In such a case the community group (or the worker) does research, writes reports, sets up joint working parties with people in the 'target system' and negotiates a changed procedure, not necessarily without disagreement and the use of power, but, with the power of argument, good presentation and, if necessary, the influence of allies.

Effective collaborative work grows best from the careful building of contacts over a long period with key people in the target system or those who have influence on them.

It is also necessary to seek out friends within the system one wishes to change, who can advise you when the time is right to act. You need the help of these contacts to use their influence in converting other people to your cause, to leak information, to suggest what line of approach might be viewed sympathetically by the top power holders, when the approach should be made, and so on.

It is also important to find the 'right way in'. A community organisation had been trying to contact the leader of the council. A contact of mine was on close terms with the leader and I asked him to set up an informal meeting. As a result the group received a more sympathetic hearing than they would have if they had written a letter, because the town clerk would probably have prevented the matter from being presented to the leader in the way the group wanted.

In order to bring influence to bear on any organisation either from the inside or the outside, you need to build up an alliance, starting probably with your closest colleagues and gradually con- verting more people inside and outside the organisation. You need to know particularly who your enemies are, and to try to win as many other people as possible over to your side, so that your opponents will have no support. You must prepare your argument carefully and use the device of the report effectively. A chief officer once told me how the housing committee had made a 'daft decision' (his words). His reaction was to write a report pointing this out, and he got it changed at the next committee.

It is best to bring pressure on the target from many different sources: other fieldworkers, politicians, professional organisations, consumer groups, central government and, particularly, from any source which has real power to influence the situation. But unless you are in an overt fight with the organisation in question, that pressure has to be subtle. Workers seeking to change their own organisation need to be particularly careful how far they go in allowing their superiors to find out that they have caused another organisation to pressurise them. It is also important not to over-estimate one's support. The forces of reaction are usually more powerful than the forces for change. Your contacts may tell you what you want to hear, at least to some extent, or they may have less influence than you, or they, think they have.

'Progressive' ideas are more likely to be listened to if they come from someone who is seen as conservative than if they come from someone with a more radical image (see Resnick, 1975, p. 465). For this reason it is necessary to find the right people to present your arguments to those who are likely to be most resistant. This princi-ple applies both in the more informal contact-making stages and in formal negotiations. In formal negotiations, strategies and tactics must be planned in detail and rehearsed with the negotiating group in order to predict how the other side will react.

Workers who are employed by large organisations, such as local authorities, have great access to information and will also have some access to influential contacts. While departmental hierarchies can often prevent relatively junior staff having such access, particu-larly to other departments, workers should, nevertheless, know how their own department works, its sensitive points and how it is likely to react. However, such workers are bound by the limitations which their own agency imposes and, since they carry to some degree its reputation, they may also use only a limited range of tactics. They may have to be very canny. A student on placement with the housing department asked the housing manager to attend a public meeting, which he refused. I advised the student to talk quietly with a councillor with whom he already had some contact. He did, and as a result the housing manager was told to attend the meeting by the councillors!

One problem with the changes brought about by the kinds of approaches described above (and other approaches) is that the gains tend to erode. By the time the new programme or changed proce-dure has been in place for a year, the main supporter of it in the sponsoring organisation may have moved on, and his or her suc-cessor may well see things in a different way. Therefore, once the change which the group or the worker wants has been approved, it must be structured as far as possible into the routine of the organ-isation. You must make sure that it becomes agreed policy, adequate resources are devoted to it and that, if appropriate, staff are in post whose responsibility it is to operate the new procedure. You will probably also have to perform a 'watchdog' function to ensure that the system does not revert to old ways of operating.

The majority of people 'tread water'. They respond to what comes at them but they do not initiate. If one is working with a community group trying to change a policy, running a major event, or is even in charge of a large department, one usually finds that most other people work in this reactive rather than pro-active way. To bring about change, a worker must personally ensure that the necessary tasks get done (sometimes called progress chasing).

When you are working within the system for change, you have to be aware of the danger of being exploited. The system may find ways of adapting to pressure without changing for the better. You may become so conscious of the constraints that you are afraid to test out the imagined limits because everyone is scared of upsetting a particular politician. You can also get 'sucked in' by the often pervasive feeling within large public organisations that it is impossible to improve the situation, so why bother? Or you may become so immersed in day-to-day 'wheeler dealing' to achieve minor objectives that you lose sight of strategic goals. Nevertheless, 'working the system' is vital in a great many community work situations.

Working the system also involves compromise and incremental gains. It is a slow process which requires the ability to see and exploit opportunities within a constantly changing political environment. But there are always opportunities which an entrepreneurial community worker can take advantage of if he or she is prepared to work in this way.

Politics, power and social planning

Social planning in community work is highly political and depends on a skilful ability to manipulate the political process.

Community workers are usually in a position of wanting to attract resources for the schemes *they* wish to promote. Thus, we often find ourselves making applications and seeking to *persuade* resource holders that what we want to do is 'a good thing'. This works best if we can discover the self-interest of those resource holders. What is it *they* want? They have to deploy their resources somehow. Therefore, if we can find ways of helping them deploy their resources to meet the needs *they* identify, we may be in business. Building power, for a community worker, consists primarily of identifying the self-interest of others and trying to meet that self-interest. There has to be some gain in a transaction for all the players: otherwise they will not play.

Another way of securing political support is to seek to ensure that your political competitors sit on your own management committee. Usually, in time, they also develop some allegiance to your organisation. You have to be careful about this though, since if they are totally opposed to your organisation they will just cause trouble.

There may be no chance of getting the resources to run the projects we want to run at a particular stage. But there are usually ways of getting issues on important agendas. For instance, when I wanted to get local authorities in Wales to begin discussing community development, I established a relationship with the director of the relevant association of local authorities. Later I asked his organisation to co-sponsor a conference on the subject. Without his assistance I would not have been able to attract local authorities.

If you do not have direct access to the people with power, establish good relationships with those who do, and they will do some of the work for you.

Social planning and personal change

Community workers should also think about how to encourage the necessary personal change in the people running the services and making the policies which we seek to influence. This is difficult to do because the worker is not usually engaged as a professional adviser to service providers and does not have the authority to intervene at that level. One community worker once attempted this within a relatively benign social service agency. He interviewed the main service providers about a particular project, summarised what they said and fed it back to them, as a result of which some of them modified their practice.

While I cannot make specific suggestions as to how attitude change in service providers can be brought about, it is clearly very important, and community workers need to give considerable attention to it. (Books like Carnegie's *How to win Friends and Influence People*, 1998, may be of use.)

6

Specialist Community Work: Some Initial Thoughts

Introduction

I have struggled with this topic for several years, and what I write below is where I have got to in making sense of it. I realise, however, that it needs more space, research and analysis than I am currently able to give. However, in spite of these limitations, I think it is important to begin to theorise about the different aspects of specialist work, and I have tried to do this below.

In considering the notion 'community', Willmott (1989) emphasises two main points. First, communities can either be of a geographical nature or be 'communities of interest' (I will also use 'community of need') where the link between people is something other than locality, for instance, people suffering from a particular impairment or who support the same football team. Secondly, there is both attachment and interaction between the members of a community. (See also, Mayo, 1994, pp. 48–68, and Henderson and Salmon, 1998, for a deeper analysis of 'community'.)

We all, at least potentially, belong to different kinds of community, both of location and interest. The core of community development work is to assist members of particular communities to come together to get their needs met more effectively. As we saw earlier, the 'generic' worker (especially the neighbourhood worker) tends to work with community groups which have a clear connection with place. Some groups in geographical communities – for instance, residents' associations – have a broad range of concerns and can, potentially, consist of all the residents of the locality. Others, for

110

example, single-parent groups, are communities of interest/need within the geographical community. The generic worker potentially works with any of these groups.

However, some community workers work only with specified communities of need. Such communities or groups usually consist of people who share a particular condition or are severely excluded from access to resources, good services and power. Depending on the context, people from ethnic minorities, people with particular impairments, older people, single parents, middle-aged unemployed men, gay men and lesbians, women, young male adults and many others, can be 'excluded' and suffer disadvantage when compared with other groups. I call these workers *specialist community workers, working with a community of need.*

Other community workers focus on community work only in relation to a particular service, for example, housing, health, or the environment. I call these workers *specialist/sectoral workers.*

It is important to add that not all community development work takes place with excluded communities or groups. The idea that communities of all kinds and consumers of services should be consulted or assisted collectively to articulate their needs or work together to improve the quality of life for their community is also a reason why some community development and related work is undertaken. In Britain, there are many examples of community development work of this kind, for instance, the work of some rural community councils, community-based environmental projects, outreach work by some community centre wardens, sports development work and community consultations by the planning departments of local authorities.

Specialist community work with communities of need: some general comments

While I was doing background reading for this book I sought to discover sets of theories or principles of work with communities of need – for instance with disabled people or ethnic minorities. I was unsuccessful in my search, at least for anything which corresponded to the principles of generic neighbourhood level community development work. This may be because community work with need communities is mostly undertaken by members of those need communities themselves, as a consequence of which less emphasis is placed on the role of the outside enabler, which is the cornerstone of 'classical' community development theories.

Having said this, in my view the main principles of work with neighbourhood based groups apply also to work with communities of need: 'starting where people are', identifying self-interest, establishing relationships through personal contact, building an organisation, and so on. Community workers with need communities have to figure out how to apply these principles to the situations in which they find themselves. However, there are some major differences between communities of need, whose members may be scattered over a wide area for instance, and neighbourhood based groups. How do you reach the members of 'need communities'? People with Parkinson's disease or women suffering domestic violence often have to be contacted via the professionals who work with them. But, do the professionals know them all? Do they trust the professionals? They may also need transport to get to a meeting. By contrast, people who live in the same neighbourhood may already know each other and meet in pubs, on the way to work, outside the primary school and so on. If one of them misses a meeting, the local grapevine will probably let them know what happened and the date of the next one. They will be served by the same elected representatives, may use the same doctor and will have many other natural linkages with each other. Just as importantly, they may well be of a similar class and culture and will share many of the same needs because of where they live – poor transport, inadequate public housing, pollution from nearby factories, the lack of play space, for instance. The members of need communities may not have the same widely shared needs, and the particular characteristic they share – alcoholism, for instance – may be the *only* thing they have in common. Thus, the membership of a community group based on a community of need may be more heterogeneous. These factors need to be taken into account when organising such a community.

The other obvious point to add is that workers working with a need community, people with Parkinson's disease, for example, also have to learn about that particular community, or condition.

Community work with extremely incapacitated people, children and young people

In practice, community development work usually means working (mainly) with the leaders of a community group and encouraging people to take leadership roles. Consequently, most community development work is carried out with adults who do not have, in general, severe personal incapacities. This begs the question as to how far community work can be carried out with people such as the elderly mentally infirm, people with severe learning difficulties, alcoholic and mentally ill homeless people, terminally ill people, children and young people. If such assistance can be provided, a further question is whether it goes under the name 'community work'.

Henderson (1998) describes three approaches to community development seeking to achieve benefits for children:

1. face-to-face work with children, which must include listening to what they say their needs are;
2. work with adults to benefit children;
3. work which is intergenerational (that is, involving both children and adults) from which children benefit.

(see also Hasler, 1995, pp. 169–82)

Only rarely, and in a limited way, however, would a worker be assisting children, especially young children, to organise to take autonomous collective action. However, there are several examples of work with young people where a community development work approach has successfully been taken. For instance, Burke (1995, pp. 28–9) describes a project to facilitate young people deciding collectively their own priorities and forming a group which realised some of these. Also, while 'traditional' youth work has often been about leisure-time pursuits, sport, recreation and so on, youth workers increasingly see their role as being to assist young people to determine for themselves what choices they need to make in life and to find ways of solving their own problems. Sometimes this assistance is provided on an individual basis, sometimes collectively. However, while such assistance to a group of young people based on the values and principles described earlier could certainly be called community work, it is usually not called this.

With communities of need which are very limited in capacity or in their ability to organise, such as the elderly mentally infirm, the scope for promoting autonomous collective action and encouraging leadership is much more limited. (There is sometimes scope for it though – the promotion and support of self advocacy for people with learning difficulties, for instance, though this is usually on an individual basis). However, it is here that the values of love, justice, respect and self-determination come in. In working with such people, or with small children, for example, an approach which was based around these values would be consistent with a community work approach, even though it was not promoting autonomous collective action. But it could also be argued that, with such groups, good community work was no different from good social work, social care or youth work. Community work with such groups, therefore, is not so easily distinguishable from other forms of work with them.

However, with all community work, there is the 'social planning' dimension, where community workers also act as advocates for the community or group by liaising with other organisations to ensure that resources are allocated, new programmes delivered or policies changed in order to benefit that group, community or category of people. Thus, while workers who are working with and for such people may have to work primarily with individuals and may have limited scope for promoting collective action, they can also benefit the group/community by taking a social planning approach.

The fact remains, however, that the people who are most usually termed 'community workers' are employed to work with adults who are capable of undertaking autonomous collective action, at least to some degree. Work with highly dependent or incapacitated people based on the same values is unlikely to be called community work.

Similarly, much of the specialist/sectoral community work described below might not be seen by those undertaking it as community work.

Some issues in specialist/sectoral community work

Specialist/sectoral community workers often find that the needs of the community or community group do not fit neatly into their sector of work. What does the environmentally focused community worker do when the community wants assistance to run a carnival, for instance?

The assumption (if there is one) behind most specialist/sectoral community work is probably either that communities are already well organised and are prepared to participate in the area of work in which the worker specialises, or that their members will readily come together for such a purpose. However, specialist/sectoral community workers often find that an excluded community is not well organised (because nobody is doing the generic community development work) and is, thus, not able to work with the sectoral worker at all. In such a case, the worker might ideally need to spend two years helping the community to organise itself. However, this would have to be around issues its members cared about strongly, and these would not necessarily be the concern of the specialist/sectoral worker. Where community groups exist but want workers to assist them on projects which are outside the workers' brief, workers have to decide whether to become generic for a time or whether, ultimately, to refuse to work with that group.

However, it is clear that specialist/sectoral workers are needed. There is no way that a generic worker can have the relevant expertise on: crime, the environment, health, housing, education and economic development, for example. The problem lies in the fact that often nobody is doing the generic work 'up front', work which needs to be done (especially with excluded communities) if specialist/sectoral work is to be really effective. Unless this happens, in many communities specialist/sectoral workers will tend to develop a 'top down' relationship with community groups, where the worker leads rather than enabling them to take their own action. Given that specialist/sectoral workers should have considerable expertise because of their specialisation, this may not necessarily be a bad thing. Nevertheless, in most excluded communities, somebody needs to do the 'bottom up' bit.

The conclusion to draw from this somewhat confusing picture is that there is a need for:

- generic community development work
- specialist community work with communities of need
- specialist/sectoral community work

When agencies and departments with no history of promoting community involvement develop programmes which are supposed to promote it, they sometimes invent their own 'brand', fail to consult the extensive literatures on the subject and neglect to use experts in the field, resulting, often, in poorly thought out and short-term programmes. They may also employ staff who know the subject area (mental illness, for example) but not understand the need for staff with community development skills.

Some examples of specialist/sectoral work

Introduction

The purpose of this section is to introduce several kinds of specialist/ sectoral work, particularly those I know most about, and to draw out some common threads. I describe these areas of work mostly without comment but draw some conclusions at the end of the chapter.

Crime prevention and community safety

Many excluded communities suffer from high crime and vandalism rates. Those in the community crime prevention business argue that you cannot do effective community development work in such communities without tackling crime as a first priority.

Sue King (Director, Safer Merthyr Tydfil, S. Wales) has this to say (I paraphrase):

> For many years crime prevention and community safety were deemed to be the domain of the police. The Morgan Report (Home Office, 1991) emphasised the importance of strategic partnerships to address local crime problems. The preface states:
>
> > Investing in crime prevention and safer communities is potentially an unparalleled way of improving the quality of life in many areas; it is also potentially one of the most cost-effective things it is possible to do.
>
> The report also introduced the concept of 'community safety' rather than the narrower view of crime prevention by offering the following definition:

The term 'crime prevention' is often narrowly interpreted and this reinforces the view that it is solely the responsibility of the police. On the other hand, the term 'community safety' is open to wider interpretation and could encourage greater participation from all sections of the community in the fight against crime.

Many local authorities and crime prevention groups voluntarily embraced the partnership message, and, in 1993, the Home Office produced *A Practical Guide to Crime Prevention for Local Partnerships* which had a significant impact on how community safety partnerships operated. This guide advocated a systematic problem-solving approach applying local solutions to local crime problems and offered a useful structure for community safety planning focusing on:

- Defining the problem via crime audit and review of current policy and practice
- Preparing an action plan – prioritising problems after appraising options.
- Implementing the project – resourcing and avoiding implementation failure.
- Assessing achievements – monitoring, evaluating and reviewing the project.

Community safety has therefore become an issue for us all rather than a narrowly focused problem just for agencies in the criminal justice system. Crime prevention and community safety are effective when they include law enforcement, physical crime prevention and social crime prevention. Projects must have a strong social dimension if the root causes of crime are to be addressed.

The Crime and Disorder Act (Home Office, 1998) required police and local authorities to create local 'community safety' partnerships. These partnerships should be comprised of a mixture of public, private, voluntary and community bodies and should empower residents to contribute to their own safety. In community safety, as in true community development, the voice of the community should lead to action. If a community seeks a partnership to initiate social and economic regeneration, the first essential step in the strategy should be community safety and crime prevention measures that will improve quality of life, reduce fear of crime and actual crime and start the return of the 'feel good' factor. *Before capacity can be built in our communities, these basic crime and community safety issues must be addressed* (emphasis not in original).

This principle has been accepted by all partners in the Gurnos and Galon Uchaf Regeneration Partnership in Merthyr Tydfil. A wide

ranging social and economic strategy has been agreed by fifteen
agencies, and the whole strategy has been underpinned by crime
prevention and community safety measures. These included not
only creating and supporting neighbourhood watch groups, burglary
prevention work and closed circuit television, but also youth work,
engaging a community artist, graffiti clean-ups and other schemes in
which the community was involved. This strategy commenced in
1995 and since then there has been a reduction in fear of crime on
the estate by over 50 per cent, and burglary has reduced by 69 per cent
after two years. Set against this baseline of crime reduction, a wide
range of community development measures have been initiated following a strategy agreed by residents' groups with partner agency support.
None of these initiatives would have been possible if the community
had not started to feel safer and taste a better quality of life.

(Sue King, personal communication
to author, 1998)

Community work and the environment

Until the 1990s there seemed to be little connection in practice
between the various environmental movements and community
development work. That all changed with the Rio Earth Summit
of 1992 and the creation of Local Agenda (LA) 21. With this came
the recognition that environmental improvement and sustainability
were closely related to the way individual communities and community organisations perceived themselves and their environment
and how they interacted with it. It also became evident that some of
the most excluded communities also suffered from the worst envir-
onments, and many of those in the environmental movement began
to realise the need to engage with deprived communities. Since then,
some organisations in Britain (especially local government, but also
some large companies) have engaged LA 21 officers whose tasks are
to improve and safeguard the environment, encourage the recycling
of waste, facilitate lower energy use and so on. Some of these
workers are working with local groups on issues such as:

- growing food
- marketing local produce
- safe walks to school
- creating better open space

- creating 'green' jobs
- creating cycle tracks
- improving public transport
- seeking to change attitudes towards the environment
- planting trees

By 1998, in Britain, a number of new organisations had been created, such as the Community Environmental Resource Unit and the Sustainable Communities Agencies Network. Such organisations were working on what had come to be called 'sustainable development'. This involved not only developing good practice at community level but also providing policy advice to the government about reducing noxious emissions, conserving the countryside, establishing sustainable transport policies and increasing social inclusion. (See, in particular, Church *et al.*, 1998.)

Community work and health

> Peoples health is determined primarily by the quality of their social relationships and the fairness (or equity) in the distribution of material resources.... . The experience of health is captured as being energised, being loved, loving, belonging.
>
> (Labonté, 1998)

The evidence is now overwhelming that poor people are unhealthier and die earlier than the non-poor. Additionally, belonging to strong networks and the absence of feelings of loneliness and isolation contribute markedly to better health and longevity (see, for instance, McTaggart, 1998, and Labonté, 1999). It also now appears that inequality rather than poverty is particularly bad for health (see, for instance, Wilkinson, 1996, or Bower, 1998). For these reasons, some health agencies are now establishing health promotion projects at local level, and governments are establishing health promotion strategies with some of the elements listed below:

- local health audits
- home-safety groups and accident prevention schemes
- anti-drugs and alcohol projects
- healthy-eating groups
- exercise clubs

- health discussion groups
- smoking cessation courses
- positive-parenting schemes
- sexual health projects
- child-care schemes
- out-of-school clubs

Some health promotion schemes organised at community level move beyond strictly health issues and cover, for instance, transport, welfare rights, and the establishment of community meeting places, thus, virtually turning into generic community development projects. This makes a great deal of sense, because it is clear from Labonté's work that, unless action is taken at community level to empower and involve people in a wide range of issues which concern them (that is by doing generic community development work!), the health of the most excluded will improve little.

This raises the classic dilemma of specialist/sectoral community work – that is, where do workers draw the line and decide not to become involved in a project because it is outside their field? – in a particularly problematic way. According to the above analysis, health promotion workers should really become anti-poverty workers and forget about direct health promotion work. Answers to such dilemmas have to be worked out on the ground. But those establishing community health promotion projects need to consider this problem during the project design stages rather than face the issue two years in.

Community work and housing

In Britain the growth of community development work is closely associated with the growth of council housing after the First World War. In the 1970s many community development workers learnt the job on council housing estates, where they assisted tenants to campaign for improvements and for the provision of social and recreational activities.

Interestingly, up until the 1980s, that work tended to take place either 'against the state' or in isolation from it. That is, local authorities (the landlords) either ignored tenant action or reacted (often negatively) to it when it caused problems for them. More recently, however, it has been recognised that council estates need the active involvement of tenants if they are to be decent places to live in, and there now exists a wide range of council-run schemes which involve tenants, sometimes even in estate management. In Britain there are also several organisations, for instance, the Tenant Participation Advisory Service, the Association for Tenant Control and the National Tenants' Resource Centre, which advise tenants, local authorities, housing associations and others about effective tenant involvement, provide training courses and make policy recommendations.

Many local authorities also employ tenant liaison officers or tenant participation workers on housing estates. Sometimes such workers are able to act as generic community workers. Sometimes they have a more restricted brief, facilitating tenant contributions to housing policy, for instance.

Some housing associations are now engaging community workers in recognition of the fact that their tenants also need assistance to organise themselves to represent their interests and to make a contribution to the policies of the association. However, within the housing association movement it is now fairly widely recognised that tenants have interests and concerns beyond their housing needs. Consequently, community workers with housing associations are now tending to play a more generic role by working with tenants on issues such as economic development, the provision of play facilities, environmental improvements and so on.

Anti-poverty work

Poverty was once thought of simply as a lack of money. However, poor people also usually have poor housing, poor employment prospects and sometimes a low self-image. They also tend to live in poor communities.

Over the last ten years in Britain, some local authorities have developed and implemented anti-poverty strategies, and the Local Government Management Board established an Anti-Poverty Unit. At local level anti-poverty strategies include:

- benefit take up work
- the promotion of credit unions
- the promotion of local exchange and trading systems
- establishing affordable childcare

- promoting house insulation
- establishing community transport schemes
- subsidising leisure activities for certain categories of people
- promoting community-run enterprises
- bond schemes (to ensure potential tenants of private housing have the deposit to enable them to get accommodation)
- re-integrating ex-offenders into the labour market
- after-school clubs
- truancy reduction projects
- provision of assistance to those sleeping rough
- health advice work of various kinds
- schemes aimed at giving poor people a stronger voice.

Just as in the case of health, some anti-poverty schemes look very much like the kinds of projects which might be established by a generic community development programme, particularly because some of them can only be developed in conjunction with or by community groups.

Community economic development I: community enterprise

Simply put, the idea of a community business or a community enterprise (the two phrases tend to be used interchangeably) is that a community group identifies both a need and a market – for a recycling scheme, garden furniture, an odd-job service, an arts and crafts outlet, a local cafe, and so on. It then obtains capital, carries out a feasibility study, draws up a business plan and hires staff to carry out the work. The aim is that sustainable jobs will be created in that particular community, giving work to local people and also benefiting the community by providing goods and services.

This idea had taken quite firm hold in Britain by 1990, by which time Community Business Scotland, Community Enterprise Wales and Community Enterprise UK had all come into existence to promote the establishment of such initiatives. Several local authorities also made money available both as grants for start-up community enterprises and to agencies to offer such enterprises support, training and advice.

In reality many community enterprises turned out to be problematic, mainly because they have been treated to a degree as conventional small businesses with regard to their funding needs. That is, they have received start-up grants on the assumption that they would then generate a revenue stream and become self- sustaining. However, many community enterprises remain grant dependent and do not reach full sustainability (see Twelvetrees, 1996, Harris 1998, and Pearce, 1993). This would not be a problem if the funders recognised that such initiatives need continuing funds to provide what might be a very useful community service which also generated some income, but mostly they do not. Thus, community enterprises tend to have a continuing need both for recapitalisation and for revenue finance (to assist, particularly, in the employment of staff) in order to keep going. To a certain extent, also, they have not always approached what they have to do in a businesslike way. They may have hired staff who needed a job as opposed to staff who had the skills to do the job in question, for instance. Or they may have carried out a feasibility study which indicated that £20,000 of start-up capital was needed but have gone ahead even though they only had £5,000.

Having said this, community enterprises often do manage to keep going and make a useful contribution to a local community. Moreover, in places where sponsors and funders recognise that, for a subsidy of, say £20,000 per year, they will get both some jobs and needed community services, community enterprises can and do prosper. They mostly have to struggle, though. Therefore, if you are thinking of helping a community group establish a community enterprise, think about it carefully, visit such enterprises, ask probing questions about how they work and where their cash flow comes from, and think long-term.

Community economic development II: development trusts and community development corporations

In the mid-sixties, in the USA, after a range of governmental programmes, particularly 'Urban Renewal' and the 'Poverty Programme', had not been successful in bringing substantial benefits to deprived areas, all over the USA a certain kind of community organisation grew up for which, by the early 1980s, the name 'community development corporation' (CDC) had generally been adopted. CDCs are community owned, 'private non-profit' bodies, but they are also businesses which aim to regenerate a locality economically, socially and in other ways. To some extent they resemble housing associations in Britain, since most CDCs have provided or refurbished a considerable amount of housing for poor people. They also run training schemes, youth development programmes, services for senior citizens and children, health programmes and so on. They may also run business development programmes, or business incubators (managed workspace), operate loan funds and provide other financial services to businesses in deprived areas. By 1997 there were about 2,500 CDCs in the USA, and they continue to form.

There was, later, a parallel development in the UK in the growth of organisations which now tend to be known as development trusts (DTs). While a few such organisations had come into existence in the 1970s, there was an explosion of them from the late 1980s. They, too, continue to form.

Like CDCs, DTs are community owned. However, it is increasingly recognised that they also need to be seen as partnerships involving local government, voluntary, private and other statutory organisations. They focus on a particular, relatively small, geographical area. They are multi-purpose in the sense that they are concerned not merely with, say, training, but with economic development, recreation, social care, housing and so on. They are now usually companies limited by guarantee because their purpose is to regenerate an area or see that it is regenerated economically, but as part of an integrated programme involving a wide range of projects. DTs often have an economic arm and a charitable arm, and sometimes these two are legally separate organisations with a high degree of cross representation on their boards.

There is now a Development Trusts Association covering England and Wales with several staff and a membership of about 200 DTs.

When they start off, DTs certainly need grants, mainly for revenue purposes. However, the evidence suggests that, over time, they are able to earn a proportion of their income through trading. They are often very effective at ensuring that a core grant of, say, £50,000 per annum results in a turnover of two or three times that amount, at least.

Nevertheless, the evidence also suggests that a CDC, a DT or a community enterprise operating in a deprived area is very unlikely to establish a self-sustaining economic initiative unless it engages in activities which bring an *assured* return as opposed to an *unpredictable* return. Examples of an assured return are:

- a large financial endowment which can be invested to generate interest with which to pay staff;
- the *gift* of a physical asset (such as property or land) where substantial income can accrue through renting out part of that asset;
- contracting with another organisation, such as a local authority, to undertake particular tasks (with the DT taking a percentage as profit); or
- arriving at an agreement with a major buyer of a product of the DT that a certain proportion of the product will be bought for a substantial period of time at a good market price. (An example here would be a childcare facility offering 20 places where a large employer agrees to take 10 of these at the full market rate.)

When a CDC or a DT runs an initiative which brings a financial return there is, of course, a double benefit. First, there is the service to the community provided by that initiative – workshops for start-up businesses, for example. Secondly, there is the income to the parent organisation which it can use to re-invest, employ staff, or undertake other useful things.

The different ways of obtaining an assured return all have certain advantages. However, a major problem with providing services on contract to another organisation is that it is difficult, through taking a management fee (profit) of, say, 10 per cent, to earn enough money to pay a core staff team and to build up reserves. For this reason, among others, the Development Trusts Association in Britain now emphasises that its members should seek to obtain physical assets (usually buildings) at no or very low cost which they can use to generate income through rents and leases. Some DTs in the UK (and more CDCs in the USA) have reached a degree of economic sustainability via this route. However, in order to generate enough money to employ a reasonably sized staff team, the asset base would need to be well over £1 million. It would also need to be in an area where what it offered could be effectively marketed. For instance, in Tredegar, South Wales, a managed office space was created at a cost of £400,000. The gross rent roll from that office space was £20,000, of which £10,000 was expended in management costs.

The remaining £10,000, while useful, did not contribute very much to keeping the parent organisation alive.

In the USA, the Ford Foundation, which has helped a great number of CDCs, does not believe that CDCs can become totally or even primarily self-sustaining through trading and at the same time benefit their area of concern. This is partly because poor people need services. And most services (youth work, for example) will never make a profit. Certainly CDCs and DTs need to be well managed and be 'businesslike' but, in my view, the idea that they can be self-sustaining through trading and, at the same time, create or facilitate integrated economic regeneration in deprived areas is illusory. While I applaud their attempts to raise income through trading and strongly recommend that they should seek to create some income on this basis, I am doubtful as to whether many will (and actually whether they should) seek to become self-sustaining in this way.

It is also important to remember that, while DTs are able to carry out some things directly themselves, they also play a part as brokers, facilitators and co-ordinators between the community and a range of other organisations, as a result of which those other organisations deliver better programmes than would otherwise be the case. They also probably attract more resources into that community than if they did not exist.

Setting up a DT is a complex process which, in my experience, usually takes about two years. First, a community profile may need to be carried out (and I would generally recommend this as a useful first step) which concludes that an organisation such as a DT should be established. Then, that community profile must be discussed both in the community and among other agencies, allowing for the idea of a DT to be debated, leading ultimately to agreement to establish one.

Next there needs to be considerable investigation into the purposes which that particular DT would fulfil, and the careful identification of the vision and mission which, subject to occasional modification, will guide it through its life. Following this, different options for the structure and membership of the DT need to be considered and evaluated. For instance, should it become a company limited by guarantee? Should it also be a charity? Should it be two linked organisations or should it be one organisation with two arms? How is the community to be represented on it? How are other organisations to be represented on it?

Usually, while a small group is meeting to work out such details, steps also need to be taken to keep both the wider community and interested agencies informed. At the same time again, resources to provide staff for the DT need to be identified, applications made, those resources obtained and staff hired. If an aim is to obtain a large asset, such as a building, then steps also need to be taken at the same time to make sure that this possibility is thoroughly explored. When agreement has been reached, through considerable consultation on all the above issues, the trust has to be legally established. Then the real work begins: that is, projects are designed and implemented. In reality, of course, work on all these fronts often takes place at the same time, and in practice, it is often best to have a project to create the trust around.

One big advantage of a DT over and above other forms of community regeneration organisation is that, as an independent (usually charitable) entity, it is able to act and, particularly, to raise finance, in ways which are not open to governmental organisations. Also, in so far as DTs are public/community partnerships and address multi-sectoral issues, they lay a basis, in some cases, for a comprehensive approach to local development.

It is also important to bear in mind that, even though DTs are organisations 'of the community', this does not mean that they will automatically undertake community development work or 'develop people'. If a DT only has the resources to provide direct services and if it does not have an agreed vision about community development, this will not happen.

Community economic development III: a redefinition

Community economic development (CED) has tended to be equated, in the UK, solely with community enterprise/business and development trusts. However, I think it is more useful to define it as any activity which increases the wealth of the members of a particular, usually disadvantaged, community. It covers work with geographic communities and also communities of interest/need. CED can, therefore, include actions by community groups, the voluntary, public or private sectors to, for instance:

• establish, run or provide advice and assistance to local economic enterprises or local entrepreneurs

- run local exchange and trading systems
- make low-cost credit available
- provide house insulation
- ensure community members get relevant training
- provide or run managed work space
- provide better local shopping facilities
- ensure community members get jobs
- create community owned income generating assets

It is, in my view, vital that CED is understood as being much broader than job creation alone because, in deprived areas, up to 70 per cent of the whole population may be outside the labour market. Therefore, they may not benefit much from schemes which are only job creation focused, especially if those jobs are part-time, temporary and poorly paid.

In one sense, therefore, CED merges with generic community development work as well as with anti-poverty work. But, looked at another way, some of the elements of CED could and should be carried out by economic development departments as part of their standard work. However, because for poor people the economic and the social are inextricably linked, CED needs to be one element in a comprehensive approach to excluded communities. (See also Chapter 9.)

Community social work

The phrase 'community social work' was coined by the Barclay Report (National Institute for Social Work, 1982) which suggested that social workers should work in indirect ways as well as direct ways to help clients, and as 'social care planners' rather than merely as counsellors. During the next few years there was, in Britain, a plethora of books, articles and projects which explored these ideas.

Community social work is particularly (though need not necessarily be) associated with decentralised forms of organisation – often called patch social work – where social workers operate in small teams in neighbourhoods (see Hadley and McGrath, 1980, and Hadley *et al.*, 1987), and it is this 'patch' model which I explore briefly below.

Social workers contemplating becoming (patch) community social workers should try to be clear about what they are trying to achieve. Also, a community social work approach has to be department-wide. It is virtually impossible to sustain on any other basis. Moreover, managers need training in it as well as field staff, since it requires a very consultative form of management.

Individual workers also need to be clear whether they are aiming to be community social workers or specialist/sectoral community workers. Simply put, community social workers use approaches and attitudes central to the philosophy of community work to help their clients more effectively. They do this in a variety of ways, but an important one is to get to know the community they work in so that they can, for instance, involve the local Age Concern group in supporting a lonely elderly person. On the other hand, a community worker specialising in the social welfare field would be aiming to strengthen coping networks in a community in order to ensure that people at risk were better cared for. The difference is that the community social workers' main concerns would be for the immediate well-being of their clients while the specialised/sectoral community workers' concerns would be to develop new or modified organisational arrangements to ensure that better social and welfare services were provided and which, in addition, involved consumers in determining those services as much as possible. Thus, the specialised/sectoral community workers would have to neglect their individual clients if they were to do their main job properly. A constant complaint made by social workers who are trying to work closely with the community is that, when an individual client needs a great deal of attention, the workers are forced to stop their other work.

During the 1970s and 1980s in Britain, many attempts were made by social workers to develop new forms of work and to add a community dimension to social work, but for every success there were many failures. One problem lay in the relationship between community work and social work. Social workers were encouraged to think that they could now do community work too. However, there were not enough people with experience of community work in senior positions or teaching to illuminate the pitfalls. There have also been other problems, the main one being that resources for social services have been sharply reduced, as a result of which, by the 1990s, the social work profession (and social services departments in particular) had mainly withdrawn once again to a more limited role.

Nevertheless, there is still a compelling case, particularly in the context of work to reduce social exclusion, that the social work profession, in order to be effective, needs also to apply community social work techniques, in some situations at least. Therefore, this work, although it hardly exists in practice today, is briefly described below.

How do workers (or teams) go about doing community social work and what problems do they face?

For such a worker, or team, once the relevant managerial arrangements have been made, which may take a great deal of time and effort, the next step might be for the team to conduct a relevant community or issue profile. The team may be most interested in data, such as the numbers of children at risk, and it will probably be necessary to research the existing community support networks: playgroups, childminders, and so on. After constructing the profile, the team needs to work out what it can reasonably be expected to achieve by working in new ways and to develop a plan to do this, taking into account all the obstacles.

Whatever plan the team adopts, ways always need to be found of keeping in contact with what is going on in the locality, by meeting with local activists or other relevant people or organisations from time to time, for instance. This work is time-consuming, and it is possible to do only so much. But one afternoon per week is better than nothing, and team members should divide this community contact making between them. There are, of course, a variety of ways of developing contacts. A worker could offer to do one session a week in an advice centre, for example. But it is important to be careful about taking on too much. That is why the team's involvement has to be strategic and carefully planned.

'Patch' community social workers soon find that they know quite a few people in the area who provide information which helps them in their work. They may then begin to see themselves as merely part of the support system for particular clients, rather than the sole agent who can help them solve their problems. Consequently, when a particular need arises, the worker not only thinks of other ways to meet it besides the more conventional ways, but also has other contacts who can help in the need-meeting process. Thus, social workers may start referring some of their cases, or aspects of them, to their new contacts in the community. And these contacts start referring aspects of the cases which they cannot deal with to the social worker.

However, the next thing that happens is that more work is generated. Through their new contacts, workers are able to offer a more comprehensive service, but they begin to realise that they have taken the lid off a bottomless pit of need. The difficulty is that there is no way of extending and developing the job without creating extra demands on oneself and one's agency. The rewards can be great as far as the satisfaction of having played a part in improving the service is concerned, but the price paid can be high.

Once outside the bounds of the normal professional relationship, we are less secure. We question established practices and try to respond to a range of needs over and above those which come as conventional referrals. We may occasionally be called off the street to advise on a problem. We may be asked to transport furniture, to arrange a holiday, to set up a group for unemployed teenagers. What should workers do when they get requests like this? Even if we say we cannot help, do we feel it our duty to find someone who can? Workers can quickly find that they have an enormous informal caseload and that they are dabbling in a great many areas, all of which require more time if they are to be undertaken properly. How, if at all, should they record this work? How do they react when an informal contact complains that the worker is spending a lot of time with Mrs Jones (one of their 'regular' cases) and hardly any with him? The question of confidentiality can also be a factor. If Mrs Brown is to be involved as a volunteer in helping her elderly neighbour, Mr Smith, how much confidential information should the worker give Mrs Brown?

We are more vulnerable when we branch out into community social work. We need to be fairly hard-headed and to have worked out what we are doing, within a team framework. Being able to say 'no' becomes even more important, as does careful planning of what we are, and are not, prepared to take on. That is why we also need our agency's backing and a clear support structure.

Finally, (and this applies to all community workers) as it takes a long time to get to know the area and build up trust among people, a worker needs to be prepared, if possible, to stay in the job for a reasonable amount of time. I would say that three years is the minimum.

Community work and community care

From the mid-1980s in Britain there was a strong governmental emphasis on 'care in the community' as a result of which many individuals with, for instance, learning difficulties or mental illness and who had been in residential care were to be rehabilitated in the community. At the same time, many large-scale institutions were closed. Together with the 'at risk' people already in the community with such needs, including older and disabled people, all this presented, and still presents, a major challenge to the caring services which generally found it difficult to ensure such people enjoyed a reasonable quality of life in the community. The approach taken by governmental and voluntary agencies to the needs of these people and groups was the development of individual care plans in the context of an overall plan designed by these agencies together. Very rarely was the question asked as to whether community work had a contribution to community care and whether assisting such 'at risk' people collectively to articulate their own needs would result in a better quality of life for them.

People with learning difficulties, physical impairments or mental illness, older people and the carers of all these people are some of the most severely disadvantaged, disempowered and poorest people, presumably in most societies. Some of them may also suffer rejection and discrimination – when a group home is proposed in a residential neighbourhood, for example. If community work is to do with empowering disadvantaged people, it surely has a contribution to make to care in the community for such groups. Barr *et al.* argue that a community work approach is important if the needs of such groups are to be met:

> The principles of community development apply to community care, both in terms of collective empowerment of care users and carers ... and in relation to the role that people in neighbourhoods might play in supporting community care.
>
> (Barr *et al.*, 1997, p.12)

They also note that 'reception into residential care often relates as much to the breakdown or lack of a network of support as to the person themselves' and that 'generally, little work is done to prepare communities for the de-institutionalisation of people and the impact which this may have on neighbourhoods' (Barr *et al.*, p.12). They go on to say:

> If care users are to participate in society, then an educative process on the rights, needs, difficulties and disadvantages they

experience needs to take place . . . . Attention also needs to be given to work with established community organisations to encourage anti-discriminatory action.

(p.13)

It can be argued [that] the success of a commitment [in care planning] to quality assurance may depend upon empowered consumers who can articulate their concerns, exercise choice and protect their interests in an organised manner.

(p.16)

Most severely impaired people living in the community are cared for by close relatives, with help from public agencies. With some exceptions, there may be little that community organisations can realistically be expected to do to help people with such severe needs. Also, as was stated earlier, to expect people with major mental incapacities to organise to take collective action would usually be unrealistic. Nevertheless, there are several successful schemes where a community work approach has, ostensibly at least, resulted in empowerment for such groups and a better service for them. Examples include:

- a local age concern group which provided a visiting service and carried out odd jobs
- 'care and repair' schemes – to improve the houses of older people
- a disabled club run by a community group
- an elderly disability and drug forum
- a support scheme for carers organised in part by carers themselves
- community based transport schemes for disabled people
- self-advocacy groups for (usually young) people with learning difficulties
- good neighbour projects
- a refuge for women with learning difficulties in which users take a leading role
- day centres run by a social services department and the community together.

Barr *et al.* also make the point that community care potentially offers more job opportunities to people in community-run enterprises, for local people and, indeed for some users of care themselves. There are now many examples of community based economic enterprises which offer training and sheltered employment for people with learning difficulties and other impairments.

In short, if you are a worker with members of such a high-need group you will find many opportunities, if you look, to work with various communities to ensure that the quality of life of your clients is improved. Also, it should be possible to take a community work approach, at least in part, to working with your clients – as is described in the first few chapters of this book. Remember though, that a community work approach is not quick, needs careful planning and the allocation of a good amount of time if it is to be carried out effectively.

Community work in situations of violence

I was prompted to cover this subject after receiving a letter from Ciaran Traynor who asked me to include material about community work in a Northern Ireland context. He informed me that in Northern Ireland the 'single identity' (that is, 'Protestant' or 'Catholic') nature of communities can result in the worker being perceived as filling a political role. Indeed, many community workers would see themselves as partisan for 'their community', and several community organisations, some of whom themselves employ community workers, have links with and are sympathetic to paramilitary organisations. Not surprisingly, such groups tend to find it difficult to obtain state funding (Traynor, 1997).

There are parallels here with the work of community workers in the Apartheid era in South Africa and in places like Columbia where workers may be working in situations of extreme violence. As well as all the usual dilemmas of the community worker described elsewhere in this book, the workers in such situations have, of course, many more, where the wrong decision could result in them losing their lives. A major dilemma for such workers is how far they may have to compromise on their values if they want to stay in a job (or in severe cases, alive!). Another might be how near they would go to breaking the law (or whether indeed they would break the law or encourage a group to do so) in the struggle against what they regarded as an intolerably oppressive situation.

For workers in such situations, although I have not been in them myself, I would offer two thoughts. First, 'protect your back'. That is, find (legal) ways, if you can, of ensuring that there are enough people around with some power, who appreciate your work, to ensure that you do not come off too badly when things go wrong or you make a mistake. Secondly, think very carefully about the possible consequences, both for you and the people you work with before taking any action. It is vital to get an experienced worker or mentor to advise you on this as you go along.

Community work and reconciliation

In Northern Ireland a great deal of work has been carried out, particularly since 1995, to promote peace and reconciliation between communities:

> It is true that social and economic projects... of themselves will not necessarily create peace. However, equally it is true that increased marginalisation will only serve to deepen community divisions. Thus the approach ... adopted ... has been to place an initial emphasis on the objectives of social inclusion and then to seek the social space for active consideration of peace building and reconciliation.
>
> (Northern Ireland Voluntary Trust, 1998)

Promoting reconciliation between differing parties requires particular values, knowledge, skills and techniques, which could perhaps be described as yet another community work specialism. Additionally, community development assistance to excluded groups often seems to be a central part of the reconciliation process. (See, for instance Gilchrist, 1998, pp. 100–8, and Ndolu, 1998, pp. 106–16.)

A comprehensive set of principles and techniques involved in this sort of work is outlined by Acland and Hickling (1997). However, assisting – say, a community group and a local authority, or two community groups – to reconcile differences should not be undertaken by a worker unless they have good knowledge of these principles and techniques. It is only necessary to mention a few of them to indicate the similarities with community development work:

• Identify exactly who the parties are and talk to them separately.

- Be aware of what role you want to take up before you seek to act in that role.
- If you take a 'third party' mediating role this needs to be accepted and agreed to by the other parties (they have to feel comfortable with it).
- Do not take sides.
- You need to feel comfortable with the techniques you use.
- Allow plenty of time.
- Do not attempt this without good back-up.
- Find out the causes, the history, what do people really feel.
- Reflect back what you hear to check that you have got it right.
- See the world from the eyes of each of the groups you are working with.
- Break groups into smaller groups if necessary.
- Ensure that all participants understand that this is a problem-solving process.
- Understand that decisions have to be reached in the full group and make this clear.
- Develop a plan – by six months from now I want to have achieved, for instance.
- Agree ground rules early on.

Working with minority language groups

Menter Cwm Gwendraeth (MCG) is a project to promote the use of the Welsh language in a South Wales Valley. Traditionally, in Britain at least, such projects have often focused on cultural activities – music, drama, poetry and festivals, for instance. However, MCG staff found that, in order to engage a wide range of residents and to encourage them to use their Welsh more extensively, they also had to engage with many of the day-to-day concerns of local residents – village hall issues, transport needs, housing needs, employment needs, and so on. Consequently, that project came to look very like a generic community development project but with a strong Welsh language dimension.

Community work and the arts

An organisation called 'Community Music Wales' has a good track record in involving, often disaffected, young people in learning, playing and performing music. Similarly, people organising street theatre, local video projects, 'artist in residence' schemes, and the like, are sometimes very effective at breaking through the fatalism which often pervades deprived communities. The potential benefits of involving people in arts at community level are well summed up by the following statement:

> Arts programmes have been shown to contribute to enhancing social cohesion and local image; reducing offending behaviour... promoting interest in the.... environment; developing self confidence; enhancing organisational capacity; supporting independence and exploring visions of the future... [However] the models of success and key factors in replication are insufficiently known.
>
> (Joseph Rowntree Foundation, 1996, p.1)

Community work and other sectors

In many parts of the UK, sports development officers involve communities in sports. One could also envisage gardening, chess, fishing, cycling or other development officers making similar contributions. To the degree that they encourage people to take action in groups these can all be called specialist/sectoral community workers. Arguably they could also benefit from having generic community development work skills.

Rural community work

People in rural areas have needs and problems which are very similar to those in urban areas, often compounded by feudal attitudes about who participates and who decides, isolation, lack of transport and the invisibility of some rural problems. Community workers in rural areas may cover, say, twenty very small communities. They obviously cannot work with all of them in any depth. Also, transport is often so problematic that it is impossible for many meetings of community groups to be held. Henderson and Francis (n.d.) argue that rural community work needs to contain three elements which are not necessarily those on which an urban project would be based. These are (I paraphrase):

1. *Working from a distance*:
   Here the worker:
   - monitors local and area-wide issues of community relevance, by reading local newspapers and reports of council meetings, for instance;
   - researches issues by identifying trends and gathering information, about the closing of village shops, for example;
   - works as a lobbyist with other agencies in order to influence policies towards the area;
   - acts as a bridge between communities and professionals, providing information and 'interpreting' both ways;
   - supports networks of existing community groups by providing advice, information and training.

2. *Focused indirect work*:
   Here the worker:
   - selects very carefully with which communities within the whole area and on which issues to focus in depth (usually on a time-limited basis);
   - cultivates and supports others, especially community leaders, in the culture and skills of community development work so that it is they rather than the worker who works with individuals and groups within the community;
   - uses existing community groups as a resource, encouraging them to broaden their horizons, expand their agendas and act more imaginatively;
   - plans and negotiates withdrawal from an early stage.

The advantage of focused indirect work is that it can easily be carried on alongside 'working from a distance'. Thus, it allows a certain amount of in depth work with particular communities or on particular issues while still not neglecting the majority.

3. *Direct community work*:
   Here the worker is able to see the whole community work process through by:
   - making contacts and building trust;
   - helping people to form new groups;
   - strengthening existing groups and building alliances;

- creating wider community strategies and using other approaches described earlier in this book.

In Britain and some other parts of Europe LEADER projects have created substantial benefits to rural areas. LEADER projects are programmes with tourism, economic development, agriculture, environmental and community development staff operating as a team to confer integrated benefits on their target areas. They represent, in my view, a good model to be copied in other areas.

See also Francis and Henderson (1992), and Henderson and Francis (eds) (1993) for more information on this subject.

Community work and networking

Today's world of hard target setting seems to leave little space for networking, partly because the consequences are unpredictable. Nevertheless, as was mentioned earlier, effective community workers spend a great deal of time making and re-making contacts both in the community and with other professional workers and organisations. Our role should also include helping the people with whom we work to create their own networks.

Those who have extensive networks have many more opportunities to advance themselves and to get things done for their communities than those who are 'network poor'. It is well known, for instance, that people in work are more likely to get a new job than somebody without work, and that volunteers often find employment in the organisation in which they are volunteering. Similarly, putting community groups in touch with similar groups elsewhere can be very useful in building confidence and improving effectiveness.

Gilchrist, who has written extensively about networking (Gilchrist, 1995), argues that networks, which are intrinsically informal, exist 'on the edge of chaos' and that, for this reason, they are easier to create than more formal organisations, though by definition, much less predictable (Gilchrist, 1997). She believes that assisting in the formation of open networks (that is, with diverse memberships) and ensuring that excluded people are networked into the bigger institutional players both creates 'community' and enhances the ability of communities to have influence on power holders. She concludes that strengthening such networks offers another way of bringing about the changes in power and resource allocation which community workers have always worked towards.

Conclusion

As I have indicated above, community work principles can be applied across many different sectors including, doubtless, some I have not covered. The work in the different sectors described above is also, it seems to me, striking by its similarity across these sectors, not only in approach, but also in content. Some of these approaches are still peripheral to the main business of the sponsoring organisation, poorly planned and badly funded. Others are now better resourced. However, many are still 'over sectoral' in the sense that they are not well integrated with other specialist or generic projects in the same community.

The sheer number of different approaches to meeting the needs of communities (of both place and need) from the bottom up, at least in part, seems to me to indicate that community work, in its many forms, is indeed an idea whose time has now come. However, if the potential benefits of these various approaches to meeting the needs of excluded communities are to be fully realised, a more comprehensive and properly thought-out approach is required. This is the subject to which we turn in Chapter 8.

7

Radical Community Work?

Introduction

In Britain, during the 1970s and 1980s, some people went into community work with a class conflict analysis and an explicit socialist or Marxist commitment to change. Such workers sought consciously to work, at least to a small degree, towards the creation of a socialist society in their practice. The term 'radical' was sometimes applied to such workers.

In this chapter I trace briefly the development of this so-called radical perspective, which, after 1990, was not easy to find in practice. I then go on to describe approaches to practice now evident which seem to be carried out by the inheritors of this radical approach or tradition: mainly equalities work and anti-discriminatory practice.

I have also included in this chapter a consideration of various campaign/contest or social action approaches which need to be part of the community worker's toolkit.

A Socialist/Marxist perspective

In the early 1970s a number of research reports into the nature of disadvantage in Britain came to the conclusion that its main cause was the capitalist system. It seemed to follow, therefore, that if you were seriously interested in alleviating disadvantage you needed to work to abolish that system! At that time, the prescriptions of socialism were, to many, fairly clear. These included:

- nationalisation (at least to some degree) of the (main) means of production distribution and exchange;
- worker (and sometimes, community) control;
- a high taxing state;
- redistribution;
- an extended role for the state in public service provision.

For the next decade or so, many community workers who sub-scribed to this ideology sought to identify ways of working which were consistent with it. Their perspective could accurately be called 'radical' because it identified a root cause of the situation and proposed a series of measures which, they believed, would create a completely different basis for society.

The key characteristic of most of the approaches to practice coming from this analysis was 'oppositional' work since one was working, in however small a way, against an oppressive class-based system and seeking to change it. This could include:

- campaigns, demonstrations and sit-ins;
- links with trades unions to build more power for change;
- creating federations of community groups to develop more power for tenants or residents;
- seeking to change people's minds through propaganda and polit-ical education.

In my view, many of those who sought to apply such perspectives to their practice did not fully come to grips with three main issues. First, if you are a community worker working for a local authority, for example, on a deprived council estate, how could you gain the space to work in 'oppositional' ways whatever these were? (Many community workers were then, and still are, told what to do by rather directive employers). Secondly, since a worker has to seek to achieve specific objectives, evidence was needed that working in oppositional, rather than more consensual ways, for instance, was more effective at achieving these objectives. Finally, community workers could not reasonably be called such if they did not work at least to some degree to the community's agenda, most of whose members probably did not share the same political views.

By the mid-1990s, fifteen years of conservative rule in Britain had changed the political landscape. Many nationalised industries had been privatised. Prospective governments which proposed higher income tax would clearly not get elected. The power of local councils and the resources available for them to spend had been reduced, and there was widespread recognition that they could sometimes be very wasteful, oppressive and bureaucratic. There was also great governmental emphasis on competitive capitalism and individual entrepreneurialism. All these were changes away from 'socialism'.

Additionally, the 1990s became the decade of 'partnership' (the word, not the reality on the whole!) in the sense that it was recognised by government that the public, private and community sectors all had to work together to bring about benefits for excluded areas and people. Communities began to be asked for their views. In this context any remaining scope for oppositional work became even more limited.

For all these reasons, there remained little basis for the practice of community work in a 'socialist' way.

Insights from feminism

In my view, the contribution of feminism to community work in Britain needs to be seen, initially at least, as a reaction to the apparently 'macho' and materialistic world view of some Marxist/ socialist community workers. Simply put, feminists drew attention to power inequalities between men and women (in particular), the need to work on issues to do with caring (for children and older people, for instance), the importance of matters such as personal growth and change which some community workers had seemed to neglect, and the need to find ways of working which were co-operative, rather than hierarchical and bureaucratic. In fact, feminism provided a kind of gender-based class analysis.

Many of these ideas from feminism were accepted quickly (in theory at least) by 'socialist' community workers (and others) and, for a time during the 1980s, it was, I believe, possible to identify people who seemed to fit the model of a socialist/feminist community worker in that they consciously tried to combine insights from both these world views in their practice. Some were 'zealots' who seemed to place ideology above the experience and constraints of practice. Others combined a commitment to their ideology with an ability to act pragmatically and effectively, recognising that you had to achieve real benefits in a relatively short time for the people about whom you were concerned and with whom you were working. Yet other workers, who did not start from the socialist/feminist analysis briefly described above, also took note of some of these insights and the prescriptions for practice which flowed from them – for men not to act oppressively towards women, for instance.

A wider concern with equality

At about the same time, but mostly independently of the women's movement, the movement for race equality began to emerge, whose advocates argued that racist discrimination was endemic and systematic in white society. However, while there were some books and articles relating such work to (professional) community work (for example, Ohri, Manning and Curno, (eds) 1982) anti-racist practice did not, at least in the early 1980s, feed into the mainstream of community work thought as feminism did.

By the mid 1980s, however, the 'oppression' of women, ethnic minorities and, later, other groups – older people, gay men, lesbians and disabled people, for instance – was firmly on the agenda as it was increasingly recognised that certain people are systematically denied opportunities both by the way public and private organisations work (institutional discrimination) and by personal prejudice. From then on, many local authorities, and some private companies, developed equal opportunities policies and engaged (under a variety of names) 'equalities officers' whose job was to ensure equality of opportunity (mainly in relation to employment).

Such posts (some of which were in the voluntary sector) enabled some community workers to act as advocates for 'oppressed' groups, to help them build their own power and act as their own advocates.

Thus by about 1990, those community workers who would have been associated with a 'radical' (socialist/feminist) approach to practice had tended to adopt as their focus a burning concern to fight against inequality, discrimination and injustice as suffered by oppressed groups such as those mentioned above, and to build the power of such groups. The narrow 'socialist' class analysis had been replaced by a wide-ranging commitment to combat all forms of discrimination and exploitation.

This focus on equality and anti-discrimination was probably brought about by five main factors. First, under Thatcherism, in particular, the opportunities for community workers (who in Britain are mostly funded directly or indirectly by the state) to work consciously towards achieving 'socialist goals' became practically non-existent. Second, the feminist critique of old-style (for example, male and trades union dominated) socialism was indeed compelling. By implication too, there was obviously a wide range of severely oppressed groups: for instance, ethnic minorities, disabled people, older people. Third, many socialists had begun seriously to question traditional socialist dogmas. Fourth, by the time the Labour Party was likely to come to power again (that is, in the mid 1990s) the Labour leadership had also jettisoned several of those ideas and had, in particular, embraced the 'market' rather than seeking to control it. Thus, whatever they believed, community workers had to become resigned to the fact that capitalism was here to stay. Finally, government itself recognised the exclusion of certain groups from opportunities. Thus, successive governments passed legislation and created or financed institutions designed to protect and promote the rights of such groups. However effective or ineffective such institutions were, their existence sanctioned work to empower such groups and advocate on their behalf.

Thus, the inheritors of what can still perhaps best be called the 'radical tradition' in community work in Britain tended to find themselves working on equality issues in relation to a range of excluded or oppressed groups in the public, voluntary and to a lesser extent the private sectors. It is, however, difficult to identify differences in practice between the work of those people working with excluded groups who come from this 'radical' tradition and those who do not. Thus, the term 'radical' is probably not applicable today in British community work, and, in fact, is now rarely used.

Community work – with women, ethnic minorities, disabled people or other excluded people – around issues of equality can be seen both as a dimension to all forms of practice and as a form of specialised community work with or in relation to a need community as described in Chapter 5.

The ultimate paradox is that some aspects of a Marxist analysis are, in my view, increasingly relevant today. The global market has meant that, while capitalism has ensured that many prosper beyond their wildest dreams, many others seem destined to have poor jobs (or no jobs), poor health, poor education and a life of poverty. The requirements of the market, we are told, mean that less must be spent on social security and less taken from the reasonably well off in tax. As the majority are not badly off, they do not vote for redistribution. Prospective governments advocating substantial redistribution would, arguably, not get elected. This is, in my view, a kind of class oppression structured into national economic and social systems in which unskilled people, poorly educated and sick people, disabled people, people from ethnic minorities and (especially older) women continue to be denied a reasonable quality of life. This is not to say that the answer is to seek to abolish the global market, nor that nothing is ever done to alleviate the situation. The answers are not simple.

We also need to recognise that whatever is done by government to redistribute resources, society's institutions and the individuals within them tend to develop systems and cultures which reinforce negative attitudes to: 'scroungers', ('disaffected') young people, ethnic minority people, women (in some situations), disabled people, older people, and so on. One extreme version of these negative cultural patterns is, of course, racist attacks which are often carried out by young white people, themselves disadvantaged, on ethnic minority people. The economic position of 'excluded' people, together with these cultural forces and expectations also often create a kind of 'learned helplessness' and prevent excluded people from developing positive self-images and envisioning for themselves a better world where they are succeeding rather than failing.

Thus, action is certainly needed at different levels and in a wide range of ways to counteract these economic, social, cultural and psychological processes which produce and perpetuate systematic oppression, exclusion and powerlessness. We look now at how community workers can begin to address these issues in their work.

Towards anti-discriminatory practice

As we saw earlier, there has always tended to be a gap between 'radical' analyses of society and prescriptions for effective community work practice flowing from such analyses.

In my view the effective practitioner seeks to examine as objectively as possible any principles for practice which seem to flow from a particular ideology, compares these with principles or theories from elsewhere – for instance, organisation theory, management theory, counselling theory – and checks out whether such principles work in practice. However, this process of checking out the applicability of various theories or principles to practice is not an easy one because of the limited time one usually has available, the difficulties we all find in understanding and evaluating new ideas and a reluctance to try new ways of working.

Those workers who have been developing 'anti-discriminatory' (community work) practice tend to emphasise the following core principles:

- justice
- respect
- solidarity
- access
- equality
- (valuing) diversity and difference

However, they also tend to emphasise the importance of having an analysis of power relations and how these tend to reinforce the status quo on both a macro and a micro level. (See, for instance, Gilchrist, 1992, pp. 22–8.) Without such an analysis and a recognition of how power relations operate and what is holding them in place a worker will not be able to identify targets for change, however small that change may be. At a practical level Gilchrist argues that community workers need to:

- recognise that the exclusion and marginalisation of certain groups is a reality at all levels of society;
- understand that we all need to find ways of working which empower and include excluded groups and individuals;
- seek to ensure that the organisations in which we work or are involved do not discriminate against such groups;
- combat discriminatory behaviour or systems;
- encourage others to combat them.

There is no exact prescription for working in non-sexist, ageist or racist ways. It is, in my view, a matter of awareness, self monitoring, particularly of our assumptions (are we surprised when we find an elderly woman as chair of the housing committee, for instance?), the language we use and asserting values to do with equality and non-oppressive attitudes. Workers might also consider discussing with each other how they go about this.

There are also a range of equal opportunity policies and positive action strategies which we should seek to ensure are adopted by the organisations we work in. It is particularly important for the appropriate culture to be set at the top, though this is difficult to do if you are near the bottom!

An example of anti-discriminatory practice in community work

As we saw earlier, community leaders and community groups can be narrow, obstinate, aggressive, undemocratic and intolerant. Effective community work practice needs to recognise this not uncommon reality. It is no service to the profession if we pretend that the members of the communities we work with are always enlightened, tolerant, respectful, insightful and so on. So what do we do about it?

Alison Gilchrist (who was white, middle-class and relatively young) helped community groups in an inner city neighbourhood of Bristol establish and run a community centre. To her considerable concern she found that, in the middle of the area which now accommodated significant black and ethnic minority populations, the community association which employed her was run largely by local white people, including several influential working-class people who had lived there all their lives. In effect, other groups (especially black groups) were excluded, though not by conscious intent.

Alison worked with others for six years to change this situation and to encourage the organisation also to address other dimensions of oppression (for instance, disability and sexual orientation). She had some success, but it was challenging work. From this experience she developed some principles for 'anti-discriminatory practice' (ADP) which are outlined below.

1. Work to create a less discriminatory situation (and attitudes) must be strategic and have time and resources allocated to it.
2. It is important to understand the detail and dynamics of the local context.
3. Understand too that there are three kinds of causes of discrimination:

   (a) *Psychological*: prejudice, hostility, ignorance, different cultural values.
   (b) *Practical*: access issues (for example, no interpreters), lack of facilities (for instance, childcare), lack of transport, access to information (for example, problems with language, use of jargon and so on), cultural requirements not being catered for (Muslims not necessarily drinking alcohol, for instance, or allowing boys and girls to mix).
   (c) *Political*: institutional and legal power, informal decision-making networks.

4. Understand that you can work in three main ways:

   (a) *Empowering the oppressed* through: outreach, consultation, targeting, creating positive images, providing access to information and decision taking, arranging separate provision, providing support, supporting 'self organisation' and showing solidarity.
   (b) *Challenging the oppression* by: 'chatting', providing training and education, encouraging cultural awareness, persuading the discriminators to change policies, procedures and practices, engaging in confrontation and other conflict tactics, making connections between oppression which the oppressors may also suffer and that of those whom they are oppressing, and identifying common areas of concern between the two groups.
   (c) *Celebrating diversity* by: being positive about different choices and cultures, creating opportunities for people to work successfully together around shared issues, organising events which enable people to meet informally (for instance, cultural or sports activities, meals or trips) and enabling people to learn from each other different experiences or perspectives.

5. It can be useful, to divide up the ADP strategy in these ways and to decide which approaches you are going to try to take, when, how, and in what combination.
6. Adopt targets – for instance, 'in five years time I would like to see the users of this community centre being 50 per cent black', or 'this summer I would like to see at least three disabled children using the play scheme regularly'.
7. Monitor progress and evaluate how the work develops, being sensitive to change and flexible in response to criticism.
8. Consult continually with the people whom you are trying to help and ask them what they want to see happen.
9. Educate yourself about the situation. (Alison had to recognise that the Muslim requirement to pray several times a day had an impact on the organisation of a meeting if Muslims were to attend it, for instance.)
10. Work out who is likely to be deterred or prevented from participating by a particular arrangement.
11. Start on the gentler, more persuasive, 'chatty' approaches and only move to confrontational approaches later.
12. Recognise that ADP takes time and resources and that the allocation of these will need to be justified.
13. Create a good professional support system for yourself before engaging in such work, because you will need to use it, and work hard to find allies.

Alison discovered a number of positive and negative consequences of ADP. On the negative side she found that she had stirred up some antagonism and suspicion towards herself, as well as conflict within the group she was working with. Some group members had drifted away. Several people had had their feelings hurt. Consequently, she had to spend time with them, in their homes sometimes, helping them work through these feelings. In the process of ADP some people's genuine needs and aspirations were neglected. Finally, some people got labelled as racist.

On the positive side a greater tolerance of diversity was created and, in some cases, the value of this was recognised. Some people were certainly empowered and began to look at themselves in new ways. The conflict, while very difficult at times, also generated a great deal of energy and opened up discussion. There was much learning on both sides and, in some cases, greater understanding.

More needs and aspirations were met. The end result was fairer access to power and resources.

However, reflecting on her professional role, Alison questioned the legitimacy of her approach. She concluded that it is vital to be clear about one's mandate. She found that:

- some black people said she was not doing enough;
- some white people said she was doing too much and neglecting their interests;
- some *black* people said she should not be doing this at all!

She was also aware that the worker could easily abuse her own power. In her attempts to change the views and behaviour of some residents she might well be perceived as disempowering and unsympathetic to their needs and experiences as white working-class older people.

Also, as resources are always scarce, it may be necessary to take them from somewhere else in order to carry out ADP.

The ADP worker needs to play a range of roles: enabler, organiser, challenger, advocate, developer. It is important to work out which one you are adopting when and with whom and to play that role honestly and openly. One particular dilemma is that, while community workers often operate with groups in relatively nondirective ways, in order to address the issue of inequality you sometimes have to be very challenging and, in a sense, judgemental.

A continuing concern is always the question of 'tokenism' – for instance, inviting members of the black community to join the management committee without the deeper change of attitudes among its existing members which would bring about and sustain change.

This work can also be very stressful and, in my view, needs to be planned with care and carried out by staff who have good management and support systems. Training in it is also vital.

While this approach to ADP was described in the context of work with a community group, the principles can be applied more broadly, for example, within or between larger organisations.

Alison Gilchrist also describes another approach to ADP when writing about the Bristol Festival Against Racism (Gilchrist, 1998, pp. 100–8). In this project she and others assisted a wide range of groups to run and participate in the festival over a six-week period (in ways which the groups themselves determined) during which process new networks were established and existing ones strengthened. The festival itself and the publicity it generated assisted in the creation of 'an "anti-racist" community' and 'the development of trusting and respectful relationships amongst all those involved' (p. 104).

ADP also includes:

- making sure that communities acknowledge and accommodate difference;
- being aware of class differences;
- being aware of language (for instance, calling an initiative a 'parents and toddlers' group rather than a 'mothers and toddlers' group);
- checking whether a piece of work is likely to discriminate against children, older people, members of a particular faith group and so on;
- ensuring that funding applications and budgets incorporate money for positive action measures;
- seeking to ensure that you contact and include people who are normally not reached, for instance, Sikhs, travellers, people with cerebral palsy, themselves, and not just representatives from the organisations run *for* them, recognising that there are also disabled women and gay and lesbian black people;
- seeking to ensure that any gains/improvements are 'mainstreamed' into general programmes and procedures;
- seeking to ensure that people from different groups find ways of communicating across their boundaries, which can result in mutual understanding and less confrontation – 'you have to have a map of the political landscape and show others the way';
- creating links between different parts of the community: putting people in touch with each other and enabling them to co-operate.

'Equality' work in large institutions

In *Equal Opportunities and the Modern Local Authority* (Welsh Local Government Association) the need for local government to monitor whether some services give less benefit to particular groups is emphasised.

Anna Freeman worked as such an 'equality' officer in a Welsh local authority. She had a broad remit to develop and progress equality initiatives and outcomes within both the Authority and the wider community. Her work included:

- working with the Police, the Race Equality Council and others to prevent and tackle harassment, racial crime and related problems;
- ensuring equal opportunities (EO) procedures were fully complied with in staff selection, promotion and training;
- ensuring disabled people, people with small children or people without much knowledge of English could use council facilities and services;
- carrying out monitoring and audits to assess the authority's progress on equality with regard to disability, race, gender, and so on;
- working internally with different departments and individuals to ensure greater understanding of the service needs of different groups;
- seeking the views of (for example) disability groups or ethnic minority groups on what should be done;
- inviting such groups to send representatives to relevant working parties and policy formulating groups;
- producing gender, disability, ethnic minority, youth and elderly policy and strategy documents;
- providing guidelines to local authority departments on EO issues;
- requiring each department to state how it proposed to take EO forward;
- providing training on EO;
- being involved in setting up a helpline staffed by volunteers for the victims of racial harassment;
- collecting and collating statistics relating to all the above;
- participating in a working party with the Police, the Race Equality Council and others to create and implement a race equality strategy;
- advising the local authority's equal opportunities sub committee;
- working externally with the equality agencies and other employers to promote equality of opportunity.

Anna (who regards herself as a feminist/socialist) emphasised the need not to be seen as a 'zealot' in her equality work. She cited the example of children allegedly being taught to sing 'baa baa green sheep' because 'baa baa black sheep' supposedly had racist overtones. She saw this kind of extreme approach as trivialising and undermining legitimate language and equality issues. She recognises that many people feel uneasy about EO and emphasises that you must make people feel safe to explore the issues. 'You can't move people on by hostility and pointing the finger at them!'

Anna outlined some of the principles which underpinned her approach:

- 'I make efforts to be approachable.'
- 'People generally want to be nice people and are afraid that you are searching out the racist in them.'
- 'Recognise the art of the possible – don't beat your head against a brick wall.'
- 'Spend time finding people with whom you can work – don't spend time worrying about the shortcomings of those you can't work with.'
- 'Quick fixes are problematic. Examine an issue from all sides before you act. If you are not careful, particular action in relation to one kind of disability may make things worse for another.'
- 'Try to discover from services users themselves what they want.'
- 'Don't reinvent the wheel. Seek out examples of good practice from elsewhere.'
- 'There is a bottom line. You don't meet racism half way.'

While 'equality work' within large service providing institutions is not normally thought of as community work, the parallels between the two are obvious. There are also many similarities with anti-poverty work within local government. I shall return to this theme in the next chapter when I consider the need to establish integrated strategies for community development in the context of local government.

Social action: an introduction

Rothman (1976) identifies three models of community organisation practice – 'locality development' (which more or less equates with my (generic) community development work), social planning (covered earlier) and social action.

In social action, one group pressurises another group to make a concession or change a policy. While social action was once associated (in Britain, at least) mainly with 'radical community work' it consists, in fact, of sets of tactics which could be used for a range of purposes ('radical' or otherwise). Because of the growth, in the UK, of a range of (often pseudo) public/community partnerships, where both the community and public agencies supposedly take joint responsibility for consensual decisions, the scope for social action is limited today. Nevertheless, there are some situations where social action is still relevant. Therefore, it is important for community workers to understand how to ensure that it is carried out effectively so that they are better able to advise community groups in that respect, if they ever need to do so.

This section may also be relevant to workers themselves for situations where they form alliances with other people and organisations to bring pressure to bear, though the scope for workers funded by the state to become involved in campaigns, even in their own time, is limited.

From campaigns to contest

When the parties involved in an issue have different views about how the matter should be resolved but one party (a community group, perhaps) still recognises the legitimacy of the other party (a local authority, for instance) to decide on the matter (for example, the allocation of resources for a community centre or the cleaning up of an eyesore) the most appropriate form of action is a campaign. In a campaign the campaigning group plays by the rules of the game, consults, collects evidence, lobbies, holds law-abiding demonstrations and generally publicises and builds its case.

In practice, campaigning merges with collaboration and 'working the system' at one end with contest at the other. A group trying to influence a particular decision may well commence with a collaborative approach and, if it is not successful, move through campaigning to contest (see below). If the campaign or contest is won (or even lost), then it is necessary in most situations for collaborative relationships to be established once again. However, any one strategy may require collaborative, campaign and contest work at the same time, which should preferably be undertaken by different people or organisations working in alliance or, at least, co-ordinating their efforts.

Walton (1976) makes this point well where he contrasts a collaborative influence strategy (which he calls an 'attitude change' strategy) with a contest (or, in his terms, a 'power') strategy. A power/contest strategy seeks to expose, embarrass and discredit the other side and to polarise the issue in order to build the power of one's own organisation and force the opponents to concede. It often involves strikes, disobedience, boycotts, sit-ins, disruptive tactics and the skilful use of the media. On the other hand, the attitude change approach involves establishing positive relationships with the other side, empathising with their view of the situation, minimising differences, sharing information, building trust and making attempts to solve the problem jointly (similar to my 'working the system' model) using both formal and informal methods.

A major consideration, if a worker or a community group is involved in a campaign or contest, is whether a powerful enough coalition can be built both to persuade (or force) the opponent to concede and to sustain the victory. Also, if the group is taking a contest approach on one issue, but has a useful co-operative relationship with the other side in other areas or needs the support of other players who are uneasy with a contest-type approach, disruptive tactics may jeopardise the achievement of future goals. More importantly, if the community organisation or coalition is unable to build the power to coerce the other side successfully, which is by far the most common situation, then its members need to think carefully about how far to alienate their opponent, and whether care should be taken not to antagonise its representatives: in which case campaign rather than contest tactics may have to be used.

As most funds for community work come from the state in Britain, this makes contest type work difficult. Workers dependent on state funding need to think through very carefully whether they can become engaged in campaigns and contests at all and, if they do, how far they can take an active as opposed to a background advisory role and how far they will take their employers into their confidence.

Alinsky (1972) mentions a range of tactics which can be used in contests, such as provoking the opponent so that he brings himself down by his own reaction. But, if a group is not properly prepared, the opponent may bring the group down by that reaction. Alinsky's statement sums it up well, ' "Power comes out of the barrel of a gun!" is an absurd rallying cry when the other side has all the guns' (1972, p. xx). See also Wilson (1984) for some useful hints about campaigning in Britain. I like, in particular, his dictum that the campaigner needs to become an expert on the issue in question.

Contests between community groups and more powerful organisations are a bit like guerrilla warfare. It is vital both to build support behind the scenes through informal networking and alliance building and to begin to get the issue of concern on relevant agendas. It is vital, also, to take opportunities through the media or public events to publicise your cause. You need to understand as fully as you can how the opposition works, who the most powerful people are, who has influence on them and how they will react to a particular strategy or tactic on your part. You need to think about whether you are in a situation where both sides stand to win something, in which case you may be able to persuade the other side without a confrontation of the superiority of your case, or whether you are in a situation where, if you win, they must lose, or vice versa. In the latter case an approach based on persuasion probably stands little chance, and coercion may be needed, though if the group cannot build enough power, it will lose.

In reality, for most community workers and community work projects (in Britain at least), the 'contest' mode is most useful (perhaps only useful) when the other side will not meet you, listen to your arguments or in any way recognise that you have a right to be heard. In that kind of situation, kicking up a fuss in a way which also attracts media attention may get you in the door and get you heard. But, generally, if you do not eventually convince the other side by your strength of argument (or, in exceptional cases win a legal or quasi-legal case against them), you will not win (or at least hold on to any gains) by contest tactics alone.

In a contest, some of the tactics you (or the group) use will be confrontational and disruptive which have the aim of embarrassing the other side and attracting the attention of the media. But the disruption should only be one tactic of many within a broader strategy. Once the council chamber has been occupied a few times, this tactic begins to lose its force, and one needs to consider other methods: petitions, a continuing barrage of letters, or processions which are likely to attract the media because they contain tableaux depicting the issue in question, for example. Vary your tactics, take the opposition by surprise, and keep the initiative. Remember though, that, even when you are involved in confrontation, the battle of ideas still needs to be fought and every opportunity must be taken to present well-researched argument, using experts when appropriate. All this takes a massive amount of work.

When it comes to negotiation with the opposition, a group needs to be clear about its negotiating strategy. In the first negotiation, group members may be frightened and unsure. A community worker who is trying to help them will have to spend many hours preparing them and giving great attention to detail. One community worker I knew took some tenants, the day before, to the rather plush committee room in which the negotiation was to take place, so that they would not be over-awed by their surroundings. Remember too that 'the other side' are likely to feel nervous. They may also be inexperienced, and there may be ways of exploiting this.

Battles between organisations are largely fought at long range with each side preparing its tactics with care. Although a hastily planned demonstration executed while people *feel* like fighting can sometimes win the day, mostly it does not. While the hearts of people have to be engaged in what they are doing, their actions must be thought out. If the group's representatives are too angry or upset during the negotiation or confrontation, they may well miss an opportunity to make important points.

Some writers say that a campaign should be fun. Well, it is great if it is, but that can be a tall order. There is no way that all the preparation, the organisation-building, the letter-writing and the waiting, can be enjoyable all the time. Mainly it is hard work. However, an effective community worker also gives attention to making the work enjoyable for the participants. The North Americans, in particular, seem very good at this – by ending serious meetings with the joint singing of an old civil rights song and by ensuring they celebrate their successes, for instance.

Broad-based organising

Alinsky (1969 and 1972), an American community organiser, outlined a number of principles for mobilising communities and waging campaigns mainly aimed at government or big business. In the USA a number of organising traditions are still using these principles.

Alinsky founded the Industrial Areas Foundation (IAF) in the USA, which, many years later, assisted in the establishment of the Citizen Organising Foundation (COF) in the UK. The approach taken by these two organisations is now generally called 'Broad Based Organising' (BBO).

BBO is, in my view, important because it shows promise of over-coming some of the major limitations of community action under-taken by and on behalf of excluded or poor people. Let me explain some of these.

Community work and the community action which it supports (or which happens independently) is both multi-faceted and, some-times, contradictory. For instance, some community groups may want a town by-pass while others oppose this. Community action can, of course, be for or against almost anything one can think of. It does not all 'point in the same direction'. Also, community action and, more broadly, the social movements of which it sometimes forms a part, are not only, or even primarily, run by disadvantaged people. The lobbies of animal protection organisations and envir-onmentalists, for instance, to say nothing of the political power of the motor industry, are usually much more effective than the lobbies which are created by and for disadvantaged people. Work to advance the interests of disadvantaged or excluded communities has to be seen against the backdrop of, say, middle England or middle America, which do not seem very concerned about social disadvantage and exclusion. And it is these constituents which politicians must increasingly appease if they wish to be elected.

In short, whatever approach is used it is unrealistic to expect community work/action to bring about changes which, for example, render the poor not poor or provide access to large numbers of decent jobs for disabled people over a short time period. Wider processes in society generally allow the 'haves' to preserve their advantages over the 'have nots'. Thus, the changes which commu-nity work/action brings about (or the negative changes it manages to prevent) tend to be modest and incremental.

Additionally, many community organisations are not successful in achieving their goals and often collapse. It is observable, too, that successful community groups sometimes use their power to prevent certain groups – travelling people, homeless people, or ex-offenders, for instance – from benefiting from locally provided services. Also, powerful community leaders may dominate other community members and discourage their participation. Community groups tend to be reactive – trying to stop a motorway, rather than being pro-active – getting involved in the planning of an effective and cheap transportation system. They occasionally spend months or years fighting a battle they are bound to lose.

The Citizen Organising Foundation (COF) was founded in the late 1980s by a group of people who had learned about IAF and BBO in the USA. COF consists of a small board which raises funds, recruits and trains organisers and generally promotes and supports BBO in the UK. Sometimes it reacts to requests to work in a particular area and sometimes it targets an area itself.

BBO works in the following way. At the request of an independent local 'sponsoring committee' (which COF may well have helped to set up) COF supplies an organiser to set up an organisation, but only after the sponsoring committee has raised enough money to employ him or her for three years. The organiser then spends months holding meetings with individuals connected to community-based institutions who are:

- committed to democratic and humanitarian values (who often turn out to be clergy, social workers, teachers and other professionals);
- committed to building an organisation representing all the community's interests to bring about change.

The organiser then sets about training these individuals and building the organisation. It is important to recruit organisations which are not single issue or party political. Church organisations seem to be best because they tend to have fewer vested interests than other organisations. These constituent organisations then pay 'dues to the central organisation, which help sustain it. However, these dues are also paid to ensure access to leadership development training on the basis that this costs money and should not be regarded as a 'freebie'.

Broad based organisations keep away from issues which will divide the community and they steer clear of party politics. They also recognise that poor people are often conservative, and so they try to take a pragmatic approach about issues which will sustain the organisation. The COF staff hold the view that it is only possible to build a mass based organisation if issues are selected which most of the members support. Thus, the organisers are wary of people who are committed to one issue, whether housing or education, disability or feminism, because an over-concentration on only one kind of issue will divide and not unify. They encourage people into leadership positions who are driven by love and have a commitment to justice and democracy.

The aim of an organiser is to build a powerful organisation explicitly based on the self-interest of the members. The organisation, once established, uses that power to get into relationship with major power holders – senior politicians or company directors, for example – a relationship which is then used to get into relationship with other power holders and to ensure that policies are changed in order to benefit the community in question. However, real power (so COF people argue) is only generated through the respect of equals. Therefore, the community organisation has to build its power through research and the careful and disciplined organisation of large numbers of people. Throughout the year most of the work is done in small action teams. Then, once or twice a year an 'assembly' is held. If hundreds of people come together for such an assembly where the 'target' is, say, a large building society, the press will be present, and, if the demands of the organisation have been carefully researched and are realistic, the power of the mass organisation, together with the media, constitute a considerable pressure on the 'target' to agree to those demands. (However, while the press can be helpful, this is not guaranteed.)

Assemblies are disciplined, run to time and kept short. Constituent organisations agree to bring quotas of followers and are held to account if they do not bring their quota. Issues are chosen which will unify the organisation rather than divide it, which will politicise the community and which the 'target' can agree to. (In the US for instance, Mayor Koch of (bankrupt) New York was not asked to spend more money in East Brooklyn but to ensure that the garbage was removed from the streets!) The main committee of the organisation goes straight into an evaluation after the assembly because broad based organisations are primarily learning organisations, and the organiser plays a questioning and critical role throughout. 'Conversations' or presentations from the platform often seek to ratify and take forward previous agreements, and agreements reached in an assembly are usually a stage in a continuing process.

In general the role of the organiser is to ask the difficult questions and ensure that the group acts democratically. If a leader is not preparing adequately for meetings, he or she will be told this in clear terms. If the self-interest of community leaders has been correctly identified, namely to build a democratic, broad based, multi-issue organisation, then the leader will respond positively to the criticism. The organiser, together with the leaders, decides who should be in leadership positions in any given situation. Leaders are encouraged to hold one another accountable and to hold the organiser account-able too. The organisers are supervised by the director of COF.

There is also, in my experience, a great deal of valuing and recognition of the people involved in these organisations.

Broad based organising seems to work in four main ways. First, the organisations which are established tend to stay in existence. In 1998, there were sixty-one IAF affiliated organisations of this type in the US and six affiliated to COF in the UK. (Several in the US had been going for over twenty years, and their numbers continue to grow.) Second, they seem to be successful in getting into relation-ship with major power holders and bringing about major concrete changes. Third, in my experience, they do seem to 'develop people'. Finally, they are able to act proactively rather than reactively. In different parts of the UK broad based organisations have taken successful action on: pollution, derelict buildings, disability access, drug dealing, the environment, homelessness, mental health services, access to pharmacists, policing, and other areas. The six UK based organisations are also collaborating nationally on the need for better access by excluded communities to banking services.

The possibilities and problems of BBO have yet to be fully under-stood and it is difficult to predict what long-term effects it will have. It requires exceptional community organisers, for instance, and the lack of these, together with the difficulty of obtaining funding is probably the biggest limitation on its growth in the UK. There is also the problem of making community involvement in broad based organisations a reality. In my view, however, BBO does seem to offer the possibility of overcoming some of the major limitations of community action described earlier.

By 1999, BBO had been established in several other countries, including Canada, the Philippines, New Zealand and Australia. See Boyte, 1984, Jameson, 1988, Henderson and Salmon 1995, and

Twelvetrees, 1996, for more information on this form of community work.

Conclusion

Readers will have to judge for themselves whether the approaches covered in this chapter, which are certainly not a comprehensive list, constitute 'radical practice' or not. The more important test is, of course, whether they are relevant and at least potentially useful for fieldworkers or agencies on the ground.

8

Community Work and Public Policy: The Case of Urban Regeneration

Introduction

In my view, a good society self-evidently needs healthy, well organised, informed communities, and public policy should, therefore, seek to ensure the growth and maintenance of these.

However, this chapter seeks to deal with the more specific issue as to whether community work can create large-scale benefits for the sometimes highly deprived communities with which community workers are most often concerned. It then goes on to discuss several technical aspects of work in the field of (primarily) urban regeneration, before concluding with some recommendations about the need for a corporate approach to community work.

Many of those on the Left who were critical of community work in the 1970s in Britain tended to argue that it was big programmes, which could realistically only be delivered by government (perhaps in conjunction with the private sector), which would make a significant difference in deprived geographical communities. Clearly, the opening of a factory with a thousand new jobs at a reasonable level of pay in a deprived community, or the provision of substantially better schools, health services, housing and so on, would be the things which would make a real difference.

Or would they?

There have been, over the last thirty or so years in the UK and the USA, and probably many other countries, large-scale schemes which have aimed to create and attract jobs, provide better education, training, health, housing, roads, leisure opportunities, and so on.

The appalling conclusion which is now being widely drawn from such programmes is that they often do not make much long-term difference (for good!) to the poor people who already live in those communities. The classic example which is always quoted in Britain is London Docklands which, at vast public expense, rebuilt the area and attracted new industries. But the housing which was built was 'up-market' and could not be afforded by local people. And neither were the new jobs which were available relevant to their, perhaps limited or outdated, skills. The upshot of the programme was that large numbers of the existing population not only did not benefit but were also, in some cases, forced to move away as the area was improved, from which others took the benefit.

One might ask whether it might not be possible, in some instances at least, for large-scale programmes to be undertaken in such a way that local people benefited. Certainly, there must be gradations between the awful, the not too bad and, possibly, the good. Surely, in some situations, an injection of the kind of resources described above could 'kick start' a development or regeneration process, turning dereliction, decay and hopelessness into hope, energy, investment, education and jobs?

In some cases such an approach has probably worked. However, if we are concerned about highly deprived or remote communities, and possibly those suffering from the decline of traditional industries, the problems of how to regenerate them seem almost intractable. New industry will not often come to such areas either because they are too remote from their markets or because the workforce does not have the appropriate skills. If a new business is established in a highly deprived area it sometimes has to draw its labour force from other, better-off areas whose residents have skills, motivation and transport. Coupled with this, the attitudes of many of the residents of deprived areas, who may well have poor educational qualifications and in some cases be barely literate and numerate, may be such that they will neither apply for any new jobs nor go on training courses which are designed to make them 'job ready'.

Traditional urban regeneration programmes have also been relatively short term. As building new clinics, advance factories, schools and so on only takes a few years at most, such programmes generally last about three years and then finish. Even if they have had some positive effect, they rarely change the underlying circumstances which enable the life chances of the residents to be permanently improved. The model which such programmes have used, I think, when trying to assist highly deprived areas is the 'business investment model'. In this model capital investment is provided which is then supposed to stimulate the creation of more jobs, services, wealth and confidence in a self-sustaining way. That model is, in my view, not relevant, at least on its own, to the needs of highly deprived communities. An alternative model is needed which recognises that the problems of deprived communities are enduring and not susceptible to the short-term injection of resources alone, particularly those based primarily on improving the physical infrastructure. Instead, effective regeneration programmes need to be embedded in a very long term community development process.

In Britain, it is now recognised that the regeneration of deprived communities has to be concerned with 'people development', at least as well as with improving infrastructure and trying to create or attract jobs, and a number of programmes are being developed to that end. However, it is still generally not recognised, in my view, that the problems of highly deprived areas are enduring and that they therefore need enduring solutions.

The permanent development team and programme bending

In the 1980s, in Britain, the Department of Trade and Industry established a number of Inner City Task Forces. These comprised teams of five or six people, with a budget, whose task was to seek to regenerate small neighbourhoods in several of England's inner cities economically, environmentally and educationally. They were quite successful (see Twelvetrees, 1998, pp.168–74). However, in my view, they had two weaknesses. First, they were rather 'top down' and, in most cases, did not involve the local community much. Also, they all ran for a limited period of time, the longest being about eight years. Second, the Task Forces did not initially have any plans for what they would do when they finished their work. However, by 1990 they had developed the idea of an 'exit' strategy (later renamed a 'forward' strategy). From the early 1990s, several sought to create a development trust when they went out of existence.

GFA Consulting (GFAC) draw out two essential characteristics for effective 'forward strategies'. First, the forward strategy needs to be developed when the initiative *starts*, rather than when it ends. Secondly, it needs to leave behind a capacity to 'bend mainstream programmes', a concept which I cover below. GFAC argue that, in the long term, the real difference to deprived communities is going to be made by mainstream programmes. Such programmes would include: training schemes sponsored by training agencies, services provided by the Employment Service, literacy work done by schools, childcare provision, the quality of publicly funded housing, and so on. The point is well made that, in highly deprived areas, the services provided by the mainstream agencies may make little positive difference to the community. There are many reasons for this. For instance, the service providing organisation may have its own targets to meet in the wider area. If it seeks to serve highly deprived people it is less likely to meet such targets. It may also be much more expensive, to deliver training, for instance, to Bangladeshis who do not speak English. In general, therefore, it is fair to claim that large service providing agencies often do not have a good capacity for making a major difference to the quality of life of residents in deprived areas.

It is for this reason that GFAC has come up with the idea of 'bending mainstream programmes', that is, working with mainstream providers to ensure that their service is improved or adapted to meet the needs of that community more effectively. (Some examples are supplied later in this chapter.) Programme bending is remarkably similar to the social planning approach in community work.

All the above leads me to conclude that the successful regeneration of highly deprived areas requires *all* the following:

1. The recognition by all the partners that, in effect, a permanent development capacity needs to be established. (As poor people and poor communities usually stay poor, an approach which only lasts five, ten or even more years but then ends may well do more harm than good.) The establishment of a permanent development capacity allows a rolling programme of work to be designed, starting with small projects which are quick and cheap to implement, building up to bigger projects as trust and organisational capacity grow. In such a process the quality of the staff is key.
2. Since, by definition, the community is likely to be disorganised and to consist of many excluded people, there needs to be an

outreach capacity which engages with people to increase their confidence, encouraging them to participate in what is going on in the community and, where possible, to contribute to community life. (That is, community development and capacity building work need to be undertaken.)

3. There needs to be a partnership or collaborative arrangement between all the public institutional actors, voluntary/private non-profit organisations, the community, and, if possible, the private sector.

4. Partnerships do not happen automatically. They need somebody to facilitate and co-ordinate them. Co-ordinators must have as their prime objective the facilitation of the partnership and the drawing up and implementation of a wider strategy rather than the narrower goals of one organisation. This co-ordinator/ facilitator must be disinterested and non-partisan. This work is also highly skilled.

5. The partnership must have staff resources to 'bend mainstream programmes' in order to ensure that the big services make a real difference in the area in the long term. This work could also involve linkages with the private sector and brokering their assistance and involvement. The partnership may (if it is a legal entity – such as a development trust – which it does not have to be) provide some direct services itself, whether these be training, housing, workspace or services for children or senior citizens. If so, such a partnership will also need resources to carry out these functions over and above those which it will need for community development work, co-ordination and programme bending.

6. Finally, in order to ensure that the partnership/collaborative arrangement has a long-term future, it is vital that at least one of the big players (but preferably several) with considerable finance is fully committed to the initiative. If not, when times get hard or when the first few years' funding dry up, the venture will not continue.

Making a real difference?

We can now see the link between 'bottom up' community development work on the ground and the contribution of bigger programmes. While deprived communities are, in part, created and perpetuated by the form modern capitalism takes, the existence of a permanent development capacity in deprived communities can help to lessen the gap between the excluded members of those communities and better-off communities. However, it is crucial to recognise that effective development takes place in two ways.

First, unless there is a long-term community development (bottom up) programme, the 'big programmes' will not make much difference and will run the risk of not meeting the needs of the poorest residents. However, even if high-quality community development work is carried out on the ground and community groups are strong, that will do little substantially to improve the life chances of local people if this 'community infrastructure' does not have major influence on the big programmes. Thus, the big programmes need to be linked to and informed by community groups, locally run institutions and regeneration partnerships in which local people are involved. It seems to me that only this combination of community development work and social planning (programme bending) offers the hope that the deprivation of such communities will, in the long term, be lessened. To put it another way, effective services will only be provided in excluded communities through continual contact by service providers with an organised and informed community, assisted by highly skilled professional staff.

Joining the mainstream

The challenge for community work is whether, after having gained the trust and confidence of local excluded people and having helped them create their own organisations, the worker or project can help them get into the 'mainstream'. As excluded people have not usually gained many educational qualifications, the provision of education and training is vital. However, for a variety of reasons, excluded people often will not of their own volition enrol on training courses. Therefore, increasingly, there needs to be a focus in community work on finding ways of getting such people on to appropriate education and training schemes and into jobs.

A project in Newport, South Wales, employed two part-time staff who initially ran playgroups and parent and toddler groups but then trained some of the parents how to run the groups themselves, which also involved encouraging them to go on official childcare training. By working closely with residents, and also by assisting with fun days and trips to the zoo, for instance, the workers were extraordinarily successful over a four-year period in encouraging local people to attend training courses. In 1996, for example, they got a hundred and fifty different people from that community onto training courses. They did this by linking very closely with organisations, such as, the Worker's Education Association, and by ensuring that the training which was provided by other organisations was the right kind of training (programme bending!). However, when the two workers had to devote their attention to other work for six months, the attendance at these courses fell substantially. Disadvantaged people may need continual encouragement to keep their confidence up and to take steps to better themselves.

Customised training

At its simplest, customised training is a scheme whereby training is provided for the members of a target community (or group) according to the specification of an employer who will be offering jobs in the area. This training is then targeted at women, ethnic minorities, disabled people, young school leavers without qualifications or other excluded groups. All those who complete the training successfully are guaranteed an interview by the employer. This usually results in about 50 per cent of the people starting the course getting jobs. (See Twelvetrees, 1998b, pp.175–8 for more information on customised training.)

Here is another example (programme bending!) which, while not to do with training, makes a similar point. A community worker in a South Wales valley, which was relatively remote from a major town, had a background in the Employment Service. There was no Job Centre in the valley but high unemployment and low morale. Through his contact with community groups he got to know many unemployed people who said they wanted a job. So he started a 'job search bureau' in the valley and asked the Job Centre in the nearest town to fax him notifications of new jobs as soon as they were available. He then went to considerable lengths to bring these jobs to the notice of local people. He also helped them prepare for interviews. But he could only do this effectively because he worked as part of a community project which had good links with the community. He was so successful in getting local people into jobs that the Employment Service asked how he did it!

Building partnerships

The last decade or so has seen an emphasis on both sides of the Atlantic on partnerships between a variety of stakeholders to improve an area. In the 1980s and early 1990s the fashion was for public/private partnerships. However, public/community partnerships are also vital, particularly in deprived areas where, for a range of reasons, the private sector often has a rather limited role.

The current emphasis on partnerships stems from a realisation that no one organisation can substantially improve an area alone. Traditionally, however, area regeneration partnerships have mostly been between the big players: local authorities, economic development agencies, the 'captains of industry' and so on. It was often the case that the organisation with the most power (usually money) had the biggest say. If community and voluntary/private non-profit organisations were involved these usually had a peripheral role, as a result of which the concerns of community members were not taken seriously.

It is now being recognised in Britain that both the community and those usually relatively modest organisations which work with local people also need to be involved in the partnership. Recently, therefore, attempts have been made to involve such organisations, groups and community representatives in such partnerships. The experience has not always been easy, however. For instance, in a South Wales town a large amount of money was to be made available from the European Union to regenerate a council housing estate. The local authority developed proposals and redeployed staff to run programmes and consult the community. However, there had been a history of conflict between that estate and the authority, and there was lack of trust between the community representatives who emerged and the Council. When initial proposals were brought forward from the community, local authority officers who agreed to develop them further sometimes found it necessary to modify them. However, they did not always explain this fully to the community representatives or ensure that they consulted carefully. The community representatives, some of whom had received very little formal education, were not used to designing, let alone running large programmes, and did not always understand the proposed financing or design of a programme. Because of the lack of trust, some quite reasonable projects were opposed and actually stopped by the community – some of its members thought the Council was merely pushing through what it wanted to see done. The situation was exacerbated by the fact that community representation at partnership meetings was not entirely consistent; on occasion, different community representatives attended consecutive meetings, for example. Thus, a project which seemed to have been agreed one month was vehemently opposed the next month. In the community in question certain groups were also in continual conflict with others.

Another dilemma for all serious partnerships relates to the tension between the need for wide involvement/participation on the one hand, and the need for coherent decision taking on the other. Obviously, as wide a range of people/organisations as possible need to work in collaboration with each other and to be able to attend relevant meetings. However, meetings of more than ten can easily become unwieldy, especially if they are considering complex matters which need to be decided in a particular sequence within a particular time frame and where continuity of decision taking is important. In order to solve this problem many partnerships establish an executive committee of fewer than ten people which meets frequently, while the larger partnership meets less often.

Another problem with multi-focused partnerships is that they take up a great deal of time, where many members have to sit through long meetings until their two-minute slot on the agenda arrives.

In essence, a partnership has to be based on trust, where a few people, at least, are in a good (professional) relationship with each other and are determined to use their time, respective skills and available resources to collaborate in order to achieve jointly agreed ends. The need for trust becomes obvious when we look at: work teams (especially in dangerous industries, such as mining), sports teams, orchestras, marriages and so on. Effective partnerships are also characterised by people enjoying the experience of creating something together.

The reality of partnerships for regeneration is, of course, that you 'fail half the time'. That is, you may jointly decide to try and establish a particular project but fail to achieve it. Or you manage to set it up but it does not meet the needs which it was expected to meet. In this kind of situation the team has to go back to the drawing board without recriminations, look at what went wrong, learn lessons and try again either with the same project or with something else. This kind of situation, too, can only be successfully dealt with when trust exists. Fosler's review of successful public/ private partnerships in American cities in the 1970s concluded that the most successful partnerships grew out of good relationships between small numbers of people from different organisations over a very long period of time (Fosler and Berger, 1978).

Building good relationships between all the parties is highly skilled work, which cannot easily be done by somebody with a strong allegiance to any one organisation. It is very similar to the skill of the community worker. The partnership facilitator's task is, first of all, to get to know all the actors and potential actors and to understand fully their positions, hopes and desires. If there is conflict or potential conflict within a partnership a great deal of work needs to be undertaken outside formal settings – in one to one meetings or in very small groups, for example. Here the worker, once he or she has developed trust, needs to be prepared to explain, a hundred times if necessary, the view of one party to the other, act as a mediator, suggest compromise solutions and so on. (See also Chapter 6 for more detail on conflict resolution.) The partnership facilitator should also be the main person who ensures that the capacity of the partnership to act effectively is continually strengthened.

When a partnership is first being established it is useful if a vision and a mission are collectively signed up to. Then, when particular projects are suggested, they can be compared with the vision and mission statement and the work generally reviewed in relation to these. In initial meetings each of the stakeholders should describe their own organisation, and perhaps their personal perspective too, and outline what they want from the partnership. It is illusory to expect all stakeholders to want the same thing. But it *is* realistic to hope and even to ensure that they all understand what each other wants. This again needs to be done with sensitivity because some individuals and organisations may not be entirely sure what they want or may be reluctant to reveal it. This process of ensuring that all the stakeholders understand where all the others are coming from may need to be repeated occasionally.

Successful partnerships also need agreed and specified goals. If these goals are agreed at a particular meeting and written down, then everybody has, in a sense, signed up to them. They will need to be reviewed from time to time, too. It also needs to be agreed who will carry out particular pieces of work to meet particular goals.

Clearly, the community cannot be involved effectively in a partnership unless it is well organised. In a deprived community I would generally recommend that a community development process is engaged in for at least two years before a wider partnership is established.

Some partnerships consist primarily of a range of players meeting to inform each other of their planned actions and seeking to ensure that all of these fit together well. In such partnerships individual stakeholder organisations often still 'do their own thing', because of their need to remain accountable to another authority, perhaps, as to how they spend their money. It takes highly skilled work to ensure all the partners from different organisations work well together.

Other partnerships become formal operations with several staff working directly for them. The steps below apply to all partnerships but especially to those which become formal organisations:

1. Undertake a community profile/needs analysis.
2. Produce a report describing the needs identified and possible projects but also suggesting options for the aims and structure of the partnership.
3. Consult widely both formally and informally about the proposals.
4. Set up a small working group to develop specific plans for structure, legal basis, vision, mission, objectives, staffing, sustainability, finance and where this will come from.
5. Consult again about the specific plans and get agreement to go ahead.
6. Access the resources, implement the structure and hire or deploy staff.
7. Provide appropriate training and 'capacity building' throughout, especially for the key partners or board.
8. Create a monitoring system as early as possible.

Above this local level, there also need to be wider youth strategies, anti-crime strategies, strategies for older people and so on, covering a much wider area, which link well with the local strategy.

Evaluating community work

Effective evaluation starts with the planning process and the adoption of goals which are as clear as possible. You need to be able to predict what 'success would look like'. But you also need to know, if possible, where you are starting from.

Measurements of what you want to change before you start are called 'baselines'. A baseline could be, for instance, the number of school children getting examination passes at a certain level. However, it may be difficult to obtain the data only for the population with which you are concerned. For instance, children from the neighbourhood may attend different schools outside it, whose head teachers cannot easily supply you with figures for children merely from your neighbourhood. Also, even if you are able to get figures to construct relevant baselines around the things you expect to change, these figures are likely to be affected by many other factors besides the contribution of your project.

In practice, baselines are rarely constructed in community work programmes, although community profiles/needs analyses, now often are. However, such analyses and profiles are rarely useful as baselines to measure programme effectiveness, for the reasons described above. The project report, if there is one, also rarely refers back to the profile or reports specifically on changes which have occurred or not occurred in the things originally measured.

One form of baseline is the 'Percentage Meter'. To construct this, you need first to get community representatives to work out about fifty statements describing how they would like the community to be, such as:

- 'local people are active in community affairs'
- 'local authority departments are keen to know residents' views.'

Then you ask groups of respondents (adults, children, older people, or professional workers, for instance) individually to rate between zero and one hundred the degree to which they believe each statement is true. You then average the replies and discover that, for instance, 'local people are active in community affairs' is regarded on average as, say, 30 per cent 'true'. In this way you build up a picture of the quality of life of the community as perceived by the community and/or other stakeholders. While the answers are obviously very subjective, the exercise only takes about ten minutes to carry out (though a day or two to prepare and process afterwards). The percentage meter shows up strengths and weaknesses in a programme, at least as perceived by the community, and has the virtue of being easily repeatable at regular (for instance, yearly) intervals. See Gibbon *et. al.* (2000) for more on the percentage meter.

In community work the really important goals are often almost impossible to measure. Therefore one has to select things (surrogates) which can be measured but which approximate as closely as possible to the desired goal. For instance, a volunteer-visiting project designed to decrease the loneliness of elderly people could not easily be evaluated. If, however, several elderly people were applying of their own volition for such a volunteer, then this 'surrogate' measure could be regarded as a fairly accurate indication of the effectiveness of the scheme.

Evaluation which is concerned with measuring concrete outcomes specified in advance is often referred to as the 'goals model'. However, inappropriate goals have often been required of community projects by funders. Therefore, in order to apply this model effectively to community projects it is necessary to undertake a good deal of preliminary work. The evaluator (if there is an outside evaluator) helps the staff to identify what the most appropriate goals are for a particular time period and then to develop the means to measure whether those goals have been achieved.

Community projects never take place in laboratory situations. One project leader is dynamic and makes a great deal happen. Another fails to develop good relationships. Yet another has particular skills or contacts and uses these to develop innovatory schemes. In another situation anticipated funding does not materialise and the project changes track to compensate. In others, new political masters may change the emphasis and thus the goals of the project halfway through. Or a powerful champion may emerge who uses his or her influence to ensure the project receives special assistance.

Many evaluations of community projects tell a story of the PRO-CESS, which covers things like: the need for the project, how it was started, what it did, what happened and so on. Because each project is unique, it makes sense for this process to be described in an evaluation. A community work project cannot be understood without it. However, as is indicated above, projects also need to specify their OBJECTIVES. This needs to be done at a general level – 'to involve more local people in community groups', or 'to provide more play opportunities for small children', for example – and this objective setting may take place every year or two perhaps. But it also needs to be done more often in a specific way – 'to establish a playgroup in the community centre in the next six months' or 'to recruit more members for a community group by the end of the year'.

The information you gather in order to carry out your evaluation should tell you whether you are achieving your specified objectives. When achieved, these objectives can be called OUTPUTS. However, you then need to work out whether the outputs achieved have made any difference to the wider situation you wanted to change. (Also, if the wider situation has changed, it is often difficult to know whether it was due to the intervention of the project.) I will take the issue of road transport to illustrate this point. A construction company may have completed twenty miles of motorway within budget and time limits and thus have met its objective by producing that OUTPUT. However, questions could be asked as to whether the desired OUTCOME (a quicker, cheaper and less polluting transportation system, perhaps) had been created by the OUTPUT. From what we now know about motorways it can be argued that they merely create traffic problems elsewhere and, thus, that the OUTCOMES from such schemes are not always beneficial. Similarly, an output could be the building of a community centre, which is easy to monitor. An outcome could be whether the centre had, for instance, increased community activity – less easy to measure. A major problem is that outputs rather than outcomes are often measured. It is also important to identify unanticipated outcomes.

To summarise, any evaluation of community work ideally needs to be based on objectives, process, outputs and outcomes. Basing our evaluation on any one of these alone will not be satisfactory. There is also no prescription about how exactly to evaluate. It needs to be worked out with care taking the above factors into account *at the beginning of* a project or programme, ideally using an expert in the evaluation of community work to help you.

In this process it needs to be remembered that beneficiaries, project staff and sponsors/funders may all be wanting something different from a project. Your evaluation needs to take account of this, and you need to be clear who you are evaluating for.

While outside evaluators may be used from time to time, a project team also needs to give some attention to evaluation. For staff working within the project, I recommend that five per cent of the time should be spent on record keeping, monitoring (see below) and evaluating.

Generally, in order to evaluate community work projects, it is necessary to use a combination of approaches: case studies, studying figures produced by the organisation (for instance, number of clients helped, number of groups established), examining records and reports, listing outcomes of the work, interviewing managers, staff, beneficiaries, funders and other agencies in contact with the organisation, in addition to using the 'goals method'. (It is vital here to get views on the project from different sources: this is called 'triangulation'.) Then one has to put the information together and try to form a coherent picture of the effectiveness of the project. In doing this, it is vitally important not to ignore information which does not fit with the view which usually begins to emerge early on in the process in one's own head about what one would like to be able to conclude! Often, research like this results in paradoxical or ambiguous conclusions, for example, that certain objectives can only be achieved at the expense of others. But that is the messy real world of community work.

Evaluation needs to be distinguished from 'monitoring'. Monitoring the work of an organisation involves collecting quantified information on a day-to-day basis to indicate what is being done – number of client contacts, numbers and types of groups worked with, and so on. To decide what should be monitored one needs to be able to 'predict' what success would look like. You can then decide what data to collect and how to collect them, which will tell you whether you have attained that success. Thus, the types of data gathered for monitoring purposes are determined by the requirements of an evaluation proper, the success of which would, in turn, depend upon the accuracy and relevance of the data obtained in the monitoring process.

As funders and sponsors are increasingly requiring information about outputs and outcomes if they are to continue to fund a programme, evaluation is becoming important. In my view, a community work programme which does not build this into its work does not deserve to survive.

While, for sponsors and funders, the most important questions are usually to do with effectiveness and value for money, for project teams an equally, perhaps the most important question is 'what, with hindsight, would we do differently?' Thus, one is learning the lessons for future action.

For more on evaluation, see Ball (1988), Voluntary Activity Unit (1997a and b), and Taylor (1998).

A corporate approach to community work

In Britain the resources to undertake community work, certainly in the long term, primarily come from government, especially local government. Additionally, local authorities provide such a range of services that effective community development at local level needs to go hand in hand with the good co-ordination of local authority and other services. In short, if a local authority does not adopt a strategic approach to community work, community work will not prosper and will continue to be the 'start stop' phenomenon which it still is in many places. In other countries the direct role of local government is not always as strong as it is in Britain. Nevertheless, I believe a general (and somewhat paradoxical) proposition holds true virtually everywhere, namely that community development needs the support of government if it is to be effective.

So, how does a local authority (or any other large public body) develop a strategy to promote and support community development? The (English) Association of Metropolitan Authorities (AMA) produced a checklist for this purpose, of which the main elements are as follows (I paraphrase):

- ensure there is good political understanding of what community development is and how it can assist the local authority's aims
- approve and publish a policy statement supporting community development

- create an officer/member structure to manage the strategy across the authority
- identify what community work, if any, is carried out by particular departments
- undertake an audit of other organisations which undertake community work
- identify the communities which are to be concentrated on (at least initially)
- undertake an audit of their needs
- set up delivery mechanisms (area management committees, for example) and engage or redeploy staff
- set up a monitoring and review system (Association of Metropolitan Authorities, 1993)

A community work strategy in a local authority needs to be concerned with how all departments deliver services and relate to the community. It is about good governance as well as citizen participation. If local authorities were seriously committed to a community work approach and sought (with other organisations) to develop integrated services based on true community planning, then this could well lead to significant and lasting change for the members of disadvantaged communities.

9

Survival and Personal Development

Surviving agency pressure and building protection

A student undertaking a practical placement with a local authority which planned to build a community centre spent time liaising with community organisations and eventually formed a community group to discuss the plans. At the first meeting, some local people expressed major reservations and decided to submit alternative proposals. But the local authority was not prepared to discuss alternatives, and the student found himself being used to 'sell' the existing plan to the residents, that is, getting them to accept the authority's proposal.

How does a worker cope with this kind of situation? Employers broadly have a right to require their staff to do the work which they, the employers, determine, though good employers recognise that their best asset is the goodwill and intelligence of their staff. However organisations sometimes seek to use their employees to control other bodies or individuals with whom an exchange takes place. This is particularly difficult for community workers because they are nearly always trying to serve three masters: their employer, the community (or a particular community group) and their own conscience. We need to try to understand how we are being used and whether our work, on the whole, is benefiting the people whose interests we are trying to serve. To analyse this correctly can be difficult. For instance, the student in the example above might have concluded that the only way the residents were going to get a centre at all was on the terms of the planning department. Consequently he might not have acted very differently (assuming he thought a centre was needed), apart, perhaps, from explaining to the residents what was happening. But at least he would not have been drawn into the process unwittingly.

Once the general situation has been analysed there are usually four options. These are:

1. conforming to agency expectations;
2. getting into overt conflict with your employers on the issue and, perhaps, resigning if you lose;
3. working clandestinely to change the situation knowing that you might be disciplined if discovered;
4. accepting the realities of how the agency uses you but working to change these.

I will quickly dismiss simply conforming to agency expectations because, although it is fairly common, this constitutes bad practice. Bear in mind Resnick's dictum (1975, p. 462) that if we do not change the agency we work in, it changes us! As regards the option of getting into a fight with the agency, we need to be sure we are strong enough to win. Paradoxically, however, the time to make a stand is often at the beginning, and we can sometimes earn respect by doing so. But workers may still be told to toe the line, and if they persist they may find themselves disciplined. They may also be 'on probation' for the first six months, which can make self-assertion difficult.

The third option is to work in a clandestine way on matters which one regards as important, to try to avoid being held to account, only to 'play the game' of being supervised, not to keep records and merely to create an outward show of doing what the agency wants. There are occasionally times when one needs to work clandestinely, but there are major disadvantages in making this one's main way of working. First, you will not receive support from the agency, so you will feel isolated. In particular you will not be getting the 'critical support' which we all need. Secondly, you are likely, in the longer run, to be discovered and stopped. Thirdly, if we evade being accountable to the agency, this means we have given up the battle to make the agency change, at least from within. Finally, if there are no records or agency backing for our work our successors are most unlikely to take up the same issues, which means that much of our work may well have been in vain.

All workers need to build protection. The most common way of doing this is to find someone with power who knows what you are doing and who can defend you if this becomes necessary. Ideally this should be the person to whom you are directly responsible. If your supervisor has approved your action beforehand, and that action turns out to have been beyond the limits set by the agency, the supervisor takes the main responsibility. For this kind of protection to work, it means the opposite of working clandestinely because you must ensure you have the backing of the people who are protecting you, which means keeping such people informed. It may also require a good deal of effort to argue the case for the kind of work which you think should be undertaken. To know how to present your case in the best way to those who ultimately control your work is as important as knowing how to do the work itself. (Resnick, 1975, is very useful here.)

More generally, you can be very exposed in this work, and attacks can come from anywhere at almost any time, including from the community you are trying to help. So, make friends with influence as soon as you start work so they will help protect you if problems do occur.

Creating the space to work in ways we think are appropriate requires careful thought. If, for instance, you have made yourself highly regarded in the agency by undertaking everything asked of you, your superiors may be prepared to accept, later, that you spend, say, twenty per cent of your time in areas of work which are less important to the agency.

Individual workers and teams should spend time carefully working out what they want to achieve both at a general level in the long term and more specifically in the short to medium term. This process, which requires careful consultation, should lead to the creation of a written work programme which takes account of potential obstacles and which can be argued for and 'defended' because it has been well thought through. Such a work programme should be produced as early as possible in the life of a project (and repeated regularly). This then gives the team (or the individual worker) the advantage when discussing the proposed work with managers, sponsors or funders because you will be able pro-actively to discuss *your* plan, to which others will then need to react. The plan also needs to be designed in such a way as to give managers what they want. If not, the project will eventually lose high-level support and, by implication, funding. Part of the role of a community work team leader, in particular, is to take every opportunity of convincing those in power (in local government, for example) that the project assists them achieve their goals. When such sponsors or power holders want things which are unrealistic or inappropriate the project staff need to engage in a long term education process of their 'masters'. This needs to be given as much attention as doing the 'real' work.

Resigning 'in time'

There is also the question of what action to take if the employing circumstances are oppressive. Sue Allen (1998) has this to say (I paraphrase):

> Most of us have a 'bottom-line', that is the point where the dissonance between what we are doing and what we are strongly committed to clash to the extent that we become stressed, dysfunctional and lose faith in our ability and our work. A senior colleague of mine, advising me when I was working for a difficult and unsupportive organisation, said: 'Leave now, while you have something to take'. We cannot ignore how connected to values and convictions our work is, nor should we. I have seen many excellent colleagues and respected practitioners leave the field disheartened because they didn't prioritise themselves over a reluctance to give up on a job that wasn't leading in a direction that benefited them or the community.

Preserving one's job

I once sat in on a discussion with Richard, a community centre warden who was about to lose his job. His project was funded by the Home Office Urban Aid Programme, and the money would run out in three months. The Education Department which administered the project wanted to transfer it to the Social Services Department, which would have dismissed Richard and used the building for other purposes. The project was tightly controlled by three councillors on the management committee who had little contact with the centre.

I would rather have had the discussion two years earlier since three months was too short a time to mobilise support. Ever since the beginning of the project Richard should have been aware that the funding was time-limited. During that time he should have produced information to show what a useful job he was doing and how this work assisted with the objectives of the Education Department. This information would have described some interesting pieces of work and would have used statistics to show, for example, the increase in the numbers of people using the building. He should also have made sure that a flow of this material went unsolicited to councillors, residents' groups, the local Member of Parliament (MP) and all other interested parties, as well as the sponsor.

Second, Richard should have attempted to involve the councillors in the work of the centre. Frequent contact with him and with the user groups might have helped those councillors to identify with what the centre was trying to achieve. Third, he should have sought to convert people of influence in the local authority to his cause. He should also have worked on other members of the management committee, besides the three councillors, to convince them of the value of the project. In addition, he might have considered getting strong user-group representatives and possibly sympathetic outsiders onto his management committee. Fourth, he should have prepared outside parties beforehand for the approaching danger – residents' groups, unions, churches, officials from other departments, sympathetic councillors, and the MP, for example. Fifth, he could have asked a sympathetic person to break the story to the local newspaper, which would probably have been pleased to publicise such a matter. Finally, having heard that there was a proposal to transfer the centre to the Social Services Department, he should have prepared an alternative plan showing how the needs of the area could be better met if *his* proposal was implemented instead. That way *he* would have been taking the initiative. His superiors would have had to fight to some degree on his ground, and he would have been building up the two elements which are necessary to change policy: good argument and a broadly based alliance which can bring pressure to bear.

An effective community worker thinks and works strategically in relation to these organisational and political aspects of the work.

The stresses of the job

If one asks community workers to list the stresses of the job they usually come up with something like the following:

- job insecurity and the sometimes constant struggle to get funding renewed;
- the problem of coping with isolation and the lack of support;
- the frustration of working for an employer who does not understand and may to some degree be opposed to what one judges needs to be done, coupled with being exposed to pressure (from elected representatives, for example) and not having a professional bureaucracy to shelter behind;
- the slow progress in work with community groups which often go over the same ground meeting after meeting;
- the weather! If you have no base in the community it is no fun to wait about between meetings in poor weather ('up to my knees in mud', as one of my students once put it);
- irregular working hours. This may be an advantage but it can also take its toll on your private life, particularly if you feel you must work long hours, as many workers do;
- the pressure for concrete results, which may be inappropriate;
- the emotional effort of constant innovation rather than routine work, and the strain of constantly having to step back and think carefully about what one is doing;
- the difficulty of having to try to please everyone and of being under many different pressures at the same time.

We need to think about ways to relieve this stress. If we do not find productive or functional ways of relieving it our practice is likely to deteriorate because we find ourselves:

- taking on too much, failing to say 'no';
- failing to choose between priorities, failing to plan, acting purely intuitively, allowing ourselves to be manipulated;
- losing a sense of purpose and a sense of direction;
- burning out;
- getting depressed and physically ill;
- panicking or over-reacting under pressure;
- avoiding difficult situations;
- wasting time by chatting or moaning much of the day.

We need to find ways of alleviating such stresses.

The need for critical support

Ideally community workers should only be employed in teams, for two main reasons. First, if there is only one worker, the work stops, at least for a time, if he or she is ill, has serious personal problems or leaves. Secondly, the stresses on a single worker are greater than on a team, which should be able to share them, thus lessening their impact. However, many workers do work alone, and the following sections are designed, in particular, to assist them.

It is difficult both to survive and to develop our work alone. We often need someone to listen to us, to 'be there' and perhaps to assure us that we are doing a worthwhile job, particularly when there are few concrete achievements to see, or there is pressure from several different places to work in ways which we do not agree with. This kind of support can come from family or friends. But we also need someone to help us stand back and look critically at our work within a relationship of trust. If this function is carried out well it can both build up our confidence and ensure that we continue to improve our work.

But how is that relationship to be achieved? Many workers have someone without community work experience as their superior, which, together with the fact that they are also accountable to him or her may prevent the growth of sufficient trust. Nevertheless this form of supervision can sometimes work well and should be considered, if only because the other options are often not much better in practice.

A model which is sometimes favoured is that of the outside consultant engaged by the agency. This can be excellent. However, such a consultant should be able to empathise not only with the community work task but also with the needs and problems of being an employee within a particular organisation. If outside consultancy does not work the result can be awful. When arranging such a consultancy a worker should take care to agree the terms of the contract carefully so that the responsibility is placed on the worker and not the consultant to decide whether the relationship should continue after the first few sessions. Otherwise it is easy to slide into a useless routine which everyone fears to break. The contract also needs to ensure that the consultant serves the worker and not the agency, so that it is clear where his or her loyalty lies. (Agencies also sometimes engage consultants for community projects, in which case it is vital for the consultant to be clear whether he or she is advising the employer or the workers.)

The next type of support is that which is provided by contact with other community workers or workers doing related work in the same locality. There is no substitute for the support which can be gained from sharing experiences with people who are in the same position as ourselves, and all workers should try to meet regularly with their peers, if there are any around. The problems with this type of group are, first, that the potential members may be involved in matters which are so disparate that they have little in common, and, second, that the group can spend all its time moaning about employers. Thus, it provides some support but not much self-criticism. Some such groups engage a consultant to help the members look at their work. This can work well as long as the consultant knows their job and there is commitment among the members to work at professional self-improvement.

Finally, I found I received a great deal of support from some of the members of the communities in which I worked. My relationship with some of them was more that of colleague than anything else, and, just as they used me for support, so I sometimes used them.

In an often hostile world the temptation is to withdraw and work on our own. That way we may survive but we do not develop. Networks of community workers are also important to prevent them 'reinventing the wheel' and to ensure that they learn from each other. We must construct a system, using others whenever we can, which can offer critical support and which ensures we think objectively about our work. This is absolutely vital for workers new to community work.

Conscious practice

We also need to develop the habit of conscious practice. Much community work is common sense in that if we stop and think carefully about what we are trying to do and evaluate it afterwards, we are able to develop into reasonable practitioners. The best way to improve our practice is to try to be as aware as possible of what we are doing and why we are doing it, which can help us identify what we need to work on at a particular time. We can also look back on patterns in our work over time, begin to understand what our distinct approach is and learn how to improve it.

There are three interlocking areas which we always need to be working at. First, we must identify what knowledge we need in a particular situation. Secondly, we may lack specific skills. Thirdly, there are our attitudes and personal qualities, which is by far the most difficult area. We may have a tendency towards shyness or impatience, for example, which can prevent us performing certain functions well. Most of us are aware of our weaknesses but may be afraid to face them and therefore neglect to work on them. Sometimes we have to learn to live with them. I am rather inarticulate when caught off guard, but I can often compensate for this by preparing for tricky situations beforehand. When examining ourselves it is vital to look at our strengths first, otherwise our confidence may ebb away completely. We can only face, accept and perhaps overcome our weaknesses if we appreciate our strengths.

There is also an ethical reason why a critical awareness of our strengths and weaknesses is important. We are to some degree, licensed critics. Even if only by implication we are criticising the status quo when we help people organise to change it. It is the height of arrogance to ignore the beam in one's own eye while drawing attention to motes in other people's eyes.

Developing personal competence

A major area of competence relates to the systematic planning of work. The way to do this, especially when undertaking new areas of work, is to write down in advance all the tasks which need to be carried out and to check these with a colleague. Similarly, planning one's work schedule with a prioritised daily list of things to do is, in my view, vital. Today there are many courses and technical aids for work planning, but to do it well primarily requires appropriate attitudes and self-discipline. The same point applies to developing appropriate filing systems, office procedures, and so on.

Our personal styles also relate to how we do our work. Most community workers seek relatively open and informal relationships with those with whom they work. However, it is usually wise to try to keep our private and professional lives reasonably separate.

Many people active in social and community work share one particular Achilles' heel – lack of assertiveness. It takes many forms, though a main one is not wanting to do what will displease other people. Assertiveness is neither aggression, nor manipulation, nor passivity. It is to do with working out what one feels, thinks or wants in a given situation and communicating this confidently and unambiguously to others. It links also with communication skills, such as making statements beginning with 'I' rather than 'you', which are more likely to defuse potential conflict situations. (For example, 'I feel embarrassed when you do such and such'.) Another dimension of this is saying 'no'. A colleague of mine only advises his staff to undertake work which other agencies want them to do if it is good for the worker, good for the agency or makes money! I once agreed to discover information for an inter-departmental working group which I thought was unnecessary because I was not assertive enough to state that if a particular person wanted that information he should, in my view, find it out himself. The assertive practitioner is able to push problems which other people expect him or her to solve back to those for whom it is a problem!

There are now many books and courses on assertiveness and related areas.

We use, perhaps, five per cent of our brains, and we all tend to believe certain negative things about ourselves – 'I can't sing' or 'I can't do maths'. We also tend to create 'comfort zones' which psychologically restrict us to living only with particular perceptions of what we can achieve. Yet, we are capable of much more than we have ever dreamed of if we truly want to achieve it.

There are now a number of programmes which can assist us to become more effective personally, both generally and in achieving what we want with other people. These programmes are particularly relevant to community workers, not only because we continually have to learn to do new things, but also because much of our work is to influence and motivate other people.

Such programmes usually emphasise, first of all, developing positive views of ourselves, envisioning desired outcomes from our actions, 'deleting' the negative programmes in our heads which hold us back and communicating in ways which ensure others listen to us. Notwithstanding its rather unappealing title, Neuro Linguistic Programming has, in my experience, much to offer here, but there are many more such programmes. (See, for instance, Black

(1994) who has produced a set of mental exercises to help develop personal power, Covey's *Seven Habits of Highly Effective People* (1999) and Carnegie's *How to Win Friends and Influence People* (1998) which is a must, in my view, for all community workers.) I believe that community workers should get to know about and consider utilising such programmes.

The importance of recording

Community work agencies should place great emphasis on recording, which is closely related to evaluation (see Chapter 8). Even if the agency does not do so, individual workers should record their work with care. If you discipline yourself to write down what you planned to do, what you did, what actually happened, what you thought about it and what your future plans are, you are performing two functions. First, you are forcing yourself to reflect, to evaluate and, to some degree, to plan ahead. Secondly, you are making a record of what happened.

Individual workers should devise a method of recording which suits them. One way is to keep a regular diary or log book. Five lines per night is better than two pages at the weekend, but that too is better than nothing. If you have a good supervisor, the log book can also be an invaluable tool during supervision because you may reveal in the written word other points besides those you mention in discussion. The purpose of the log book is largely for training and reflection. It is also sometimes worth doing a 'process recording' of one meeting you attend and examining it carefully afterwards. This is a recording which covers chronologically, and in detail, everything that happened, including your thoughts and feelings, as well as non-verbal communication.

The achievements of community work are by no means self-evident, and workers have a responsibility to their employers to show how they are spending their time and what, if anything, they are achieving. At the beginning of a piece of work the worker should try to predict what a successful outcome would look like in, say, three months time – to have recruited ten members for a group, or to have organised a public meeting, for example (though many goals are less concrete than this). At the end of the period, as well as describing what he or she did and what happened, the worker can perhaps show that the goal adopted earlier had been met.

Workers should provide their employers with summaries of all their work on at least a quarterly basis. I say 'summaries' since, to be of use, records must be retrievable. Every so often the record should also contain a review of the stage which the activity has reached, and a consideration of the worker's role including, for example, whether he or she should become more involved or begin withdrawing. This method of recording forces us to think about whether we have our priorities right.

When considering recording, community workers are likely to think, principally, of recording only their work with community groups, but there are many aspects of our work which are neglected if we only do this. For example, in a project in which I worked, we developed a community contact-making scheme which needed careful monitoring. At another stage, a major piece of my work was to try to establish better relations with local schools. Ways need to be found of recording these kinds of work activities.

When you are preparing to leave your job, you must pay attention to bringing your records up to date in order to help your successor decide priorities. You need to summarise the stage you have reached with each piece of work and suggest objectives which he or she might wish to consider. It can also help to leave one's successor a list of contacts with a few comments on their position in the community and ways these people might help or hinder his or her work. Finally, we need to 'debrief' and reflect on our experiences when we leave a position so that we do not take old baggage into new positions.

Afterword

Community work, or community development as it is more commonly called on a world-wide basis, especially in the former British colonies, seems always to be the bridesmaid (at best) and never the bride. In Britain and indeed the USA there was a relatively brief flowering of the profession from the late 1960s with books, training courses, projects and whole programmes (the Poverty Programme in the USA and the (national) Community Development Projects – CDPs – in the UK, for instance). But by the mid-1980s most of that had disappeared, even though governments of all hues still ran a range of urban and rural development programmes.

In my view community work has not prospered as a profession in Britain, at least in part, because many community workers did not deliver much, while some of them made a great deal of noise and gave a lot of trouble to the authorities. Since most community development work is funded ultimately by the state it requires a great deal of skill to 'speak truth to power' and to hold on to one's job. At the same time quite a few community workers in Britain were somewhat anarchistic and therefore resisted moves to set up the institutions which give solidity to an emerging profession. These characteristics of at least some community workers both affected and were affected by the position of potential sponsors. That is, those who were in a position to fund community work tended not to appreciate the value of having well-organised communities which could help themselves collectively, collaborate with mainstream service providers and work in other ways to improve the quality of life at local level, especially if what they said and did was uncomfortable. Even if these potential funders of community work did appreciate the need for organised communities, they tended not to understand the essential and highly skilled role which community workers had to play in order to create and support such communities, especially in deprived areas. That is, the *indirect* approach of a worker facilitating others to achieve something was not generally understood, particularly during the era of hard target setting which came in strongly during the Thatcher/Reagan years. A related problem has been that the concerns of an organised community will not fit neatly into the responsibilities of any one service department, making community work difficult to fund.

These two sets of factors meant both that community workers were never really given the chance to show how community work needed to be a central element in public policy if such policy was to be fully effective and that they tended to 'blow' any such opportunities when they did arise.

There has been a slow recognition in Britain that urban and rural regeneration need well-organised, informed and representative community organisations which are also committed to humanitarian values. Gradually, renewal programmes are incorporating mechanisms which are supposed to create and support such organisations. However, the knowledge, values, skills and principles of community development work which began to be seriously developed in the 1970s are not, on the whole, known (or even known of) by, I would say, most of those in the regeneration business. Yet, 'reinventing the wheel' is painful and slow. As a society we are, I hope, approaching a new paradigm (or at least the understanding of it) that assisting people as individuals and groups to work out for themselves what they want and to take some responsibility themselves to get it (with all the limitations, problems and paradoxes this involves) is, in the end, the most effective way to ensure the development of an active and informed citizenry, which is one of the things governments say they want. Another dimension of this is the need for people to play 'change agent' roles in public services.

In such processes the facilitative skills of community workers will be vital not only for those for whom it is a full-time profession but, in a sense, for everybody. The skills of community work are thus an idea, in effect, for all time. I hope this book has played a part in keeping this tradition and the skills relating to it alive.

By the way, community work can also be great fun; make sure you have some!

Bibliography

Acland, A. and Hickling, A. (1997) *Enabling Stakeholder Dialogue: Training for Facilitators, Mediators and Process Managers – Course Handbook*, London, Environment Council.

Alinsky, S. D. (1969), *Reveille for Radicals*, New York, Vintage Books.

Alinsky, S. D. (1972) *Rules for Radicals: A Pragmatic Primer for Realistic Radicals*, New York, Vintage Books.

Allen, S. (1998) *Resigning in Time*, London, personal communication to author.

Armstrong, J. (1998) 'Towards a Plan for Capacity Building in the UK', in A. Twelvetrees (ed.), *Community Economic Development: Rhetoric or Reality?*, London, Community Development Foundation, pp. 240–5.

Armstrong, J., Hudson, P., Key, M., Whittaker, J. and Whittaker, M. (1976) *Community Work through a Community Newspaper*, London, Community Projects Foundation.

Association of Metropolitan Authorities (1993) *Local Authorities and Community Development: A Strategic Opportunity for the 1990s*, London.

Astin, B. (1979) 'Linking an Information Centre to Community Development', in M. Dungate *et al.* (eds), *Collective Action*, London, Association of Community Workers/Community Projects Foundation.

Ball, M. (1988) *Evaluation in the Voluntary Sector*, London, Forbes Trust.

Barr, A., Drysdale, J. and Henderson, P. (1997) *Towards Caring Communities: Community Development and Community Care – An Introductory Training Pack*, Brighton, Pavilion Publications and Joseph Rowntree Foundation.

Black, J. (1994) *Mindstore, the Ultimate Mental Fitness Programme*, London, Thorsons.

Bower, M. (1998) 'Check Your Postcode for Health', *Western Mail*, Cardiff, 4 September, p.4.

Boyte, H. C. (1984) 'Empowerment', in H. C. Boyte (ed.), *Community is Possible*, London, Harper and Row, pp. 125–59.

Brager, G. and Holloway, S. (1978) *Changing Human Service Organizations*, New York, Free Press.

Burke, T. (1995) 'Making Plans for Alnwick', *Young People Now*, July, pp. 28–9.

Carnegie, D. (1998) *How to Win Friends and Influence People*, revised edition, London, Vermillion.

Church, C., Cade, A. and Grant, A. (1998) *An Environment for Everyone; Social Exclusion, Poverty and Environmental Action*, London, Community Development Foundation.

Corina, L. (1977) *Oldham CDP: An Assessment of its Impact and Influence on the Local Authority*, University of York.

Covey, S. R. (1999) *Seven Habits of Highly Effective People; Powerful Lessons on Personal Change*, London, Simon and Shuster.

Edwards, K. (1984) 'Collective Working in a Small Non-Statutory Organisation', *MDU Bulletin*, July, no. 3/4, London, National Council for Voluntary Organisations.

Forbes, D. (1998) *Voluntary but not Amateur: Guide to the Law for Voluntary Organisations and Community Groups*, London, Voluntary Service Council.

Fosler, R. S. and Berger, R. A. (1982) *Public Private Partnerships in American Cities*, Lexington, Lexington Books.

Francis, D. and Henderson, P. (1992) *Working with Rural Communities*, Basingstoke, Macmillan.

G. F. A. Consulting (1986) *Lessons from Inner City Task Force Experience: Good Practice Guide I: Designing Forward Strategies*, Bishop's Stortford.

Gallagher, A. (1977) 'Women and Community Work', in M. Mayo, (ed.), *Women in the Community*, London, Routledge, pp. 121–40.

Gibbon, R., Thomas, A. and Twelvetrees, A. (forthcoming) *Evaluating Community Projects: New Options with the Percentage Meter*, London, Community Development Foundation.

Gilchrist, A. (1992) 'The Revolution of Everyday Life Revisited: Towards an Anti Discriminatory Praxis for Community Work', *Social Action*, vol. 1, no. 1, pp. 22–8.

Gilchrist, A. (1995) *Community Development and Networking*, London, Community Development Foundation.

Gilchrist, A. (1997) *Chaos in the Community: The Emergence of Voluntary Associations and Collective Action* (unpublished initial draft, 21/7).

Gilchrist, A. (1998) 'A More Excellent Way: Developing Coalition and Consensus through Informal Networking', *Community Development Journal*, 2/4, pp. 100–8.

Goetschius, G. (1969) *Working with Community Groups*, London, Routledge.

Goleman, D. (1996) *Emotional Intelligence: Why It Can Matter More Than IQ*, London, Bloomsbury.

Hadley, R. and McGrath, M. (eds) (1980) *Going Local*, Occasional Paper One, London, Bedford Square Press.

Hadley, R., Cooper, M., Dale, P. and Stacey, G. (1987) *A Community Social Worker's Handbook*, London, Tavistock.

Harris, K. (1998) 'Some Problems in Community Enterprise and Community Economic Development', in A. Twelvetrees (ed.), *Community Economic Development: Rhetoric or Reality*? London, Community Development Foundation, pp. 36–42.

Hasler, J. (1995)'Belonging and Becoming: The Child Growing up in Community' in P. Henderson (ed.) *Children and Communities*, London, Pluto Press, pp. 169–82.

Hawtin, M., Hughes, G. and Percy Smith, J. (1994) *Auditing Social Needs*, Milton Keynes, Open University Press.

Henderson, P. (1998) 'Children, Communities and Community Development', transcript of talk to National Playworkers Conference, Leeds, Community Development Foundation.

Henderson, P. and Francis, D. (eds) (1993) *Rural Action, A Collection of Community Work Case Studies*, London, Pluto.

Henderson, P. and Francis, D. (n.d.) *A Rural Community Work Model – Summary*, London, Community Development Foundation.

Henderson, P. and Salmon, H. (1995) *Community Organising: the UK Context*, London, Community Development Foundation/Churches Community Work Alliance.

Henderson, P. and Salmon, H. (1998) *Signposts to Local Democracy: Local Governance, Communitarianism and Community Development*, London, Community Development Foundation.

Henderson, P. and Thomas, D. N. (1987) *Skills in Neighbourhood Work*, 2nd edition, London, Allen & Unwin.

Holloway, C. and Otto, S. (1985) *Getting Organised; A Handbook for Non-Statutory Organisations*, London, Bedford Square Press.

Home Office (1998) *Crime and Disorder Act*, London.

Home Office (1993) *Practical Guide to Crime Prevention for Local Partnerships*, London.

Home Office (1991) *Safer Communities: The Local Delivery of Crime Prevention through the Partnership Approach – the Morgan Report*, London.

Hyatt, J. and Skinner, S. (1997) *Calling in the Specialist: Using Consultancy Methods with Community Organisations*, London, Community Development Foundation.

Jameson, N. (1988) 'Organizing for a Change', *Christian Action Journal*, Autumn.

Joseph Rowntree Foundation (1996) *Art of Regeneration: Urban Renewal through Cultural Activity*, Social Policy Summary 8, York.

Kelly, A. (1993) *Learning to Build Community* (unpublished draft) Brisbane.

Kelly, A. and Sewell, S. (1996) *With Head, Heart and Hand: Dimensions of Community Building*, Fourth Edition, Brisbane, Boolarong Publications.

King, S. (1998) (Personal communication to author).

Labonté, R. (1998) Lecture to Health Promotion Wales, Cardiff.

Labonté, R. (1999) *Developing Community Health in Wales: a Community Development Approach to Health Promotion*, Cardiff, Health Promotion Wales.

Landry, C., Morely, D., Southwood, R. and Wright, P. (1985) *What a Way to Run a Railroad*, London, Comedia.

Levin, P. (1981) 'Opening up the Planning Process', in P. Henderson, and D.N. Thomas, (eds), *Readings in Community Work*, London, Allen and Unwin, 108–14.

Lowndes, B. (1982) *Making News: Producing a Community Newspaper*, London, National Federation of Community Organisations.

Mayo, M. (1994) 'The Shifting Concept of Community', in *Communities and Caring: A Mixed Economy of Welfare*, Basingstoke, Macmillan.

McTaggart, L. (1998) 'Second Opinion – about Heart Disease', *Observer*, 5 July, London.

National Institute for Social Work (1982) *Social Workers: Their Role and Tasks – the Barclay Report*, London, National Institute for Social Work/ Bedford Square Press.

Ndolu, T. (1998) 'Conflict Management and Peace Building through Community Development', *Community Development Journal*, vol. 33, no. 2, April, pp. 106–16.

Northern Ireland Voluntary Trust (*c.* 1998) *Taking Risks for Peace: a Mid Term Review by an Intermediary Funding Body of the EU Peace Process*, Belfast, Northern Ireland Voluntary Trust.

Nugent, J. (1998) 'Building Capacity for Community Based Development', in A. Twelvetrees, (ed.), *Community Economic Development: Rhetoric or Reality?*, London, Community Development Foundation.

Nye, N. (1998) 'Building the Capacity of CDCs: A Model for Intermediary Funding', in A. Twelvetrees, (ed.), *Community Economic Development: Rhetoric or Reality?*, London, Community Development Foundation.

Ohri, A., Manning, B. and Curno, P. (eds) (1982) *Community Work and Racism*, London, Association of Community Workers/Routledge.

Pearce, J. (1993) *At the Heart of the Community Economy: Community Enterprise in a Changing World*, London, Gulbenkian Foundation.

Peters, T. J. and Austin, A. (1985) *A Passion for Excellence*, London, Collins.

Peters, T. J. and Waterman, R.H. (1982) *In Search of Excellence: Lessons from America's Best Run Companies*, New York, Harper and Row.

Resnick, H. (1975) 'The Professional: Pro-active Decision Making in the Organisation', *Social Work Today*, Vol. 6, no. 15, 30/10, pp. 462–7.

Resnick, H. and Patti, R. (1980) *Change from Within: Humanizing Social Welfare Organizations*, Philadelphia, Temple University Press.

Rothman, J. (1976) 'Three Models of Community Organization Practice', in F. M. Cox *et al.* (eds), *Strategies of Community Organization*, Illinois, F. E. Peacock, pp. 22–38.

Simpson, T. (1995a) 'A Checklist for Community Enterprise Training' (Unpublished paper), Wales, Community Development Foundation.

Simpson, T. (1995b) 'What Do We Do Now; The Brief Guide to Project Exiting' (Unpublished paper), Wales, Community Development Foundation.

Skinner, S. (1997) *Building Community Strengths: A Resource Book on Capacity Building*, London, Community Development Foundation.

Smiley, C. (1982) 'Managing Agreement; the Abilene Paradox', *Community Development Journal*, Jan. vol. 17., No. 1, pp. 54–68.

Smith, J. (1979) 'An Advice Centre in a Community Work Project', in M. Dungate *et al.* (eds), *Collective Action*, London, Association of Community Workers/Community Projects Foundation.

Smith, L. (1981) 'A model for the Development of Public Participation in Local Authority Decision Making', and 'Public Participation in Islington – a Case Study', both in D. Jones and L. Smith (eds), *Deprivation and Community Action*, London, Association of Community Workers/ Routledge).

Specht, H. (1975) 'Disruptive Tactics', in R.M. Kramer and H. Specht (eds), *Readings in Community Organization Practice*, Prentice Hall, pp. 336–48.

Stanton, A. (1989) *Invitation to Self Management*, Middlesex, Dab Hand Press.

Taylor, M. (1998) *Evaluating Community Projects for European Funding*, Caerphilly, Wales Council for Voluntary Action.

Thomas, A. (1997) *The Newport Resource Centre Duffryn Project: An Evaluation*, London, Community Development Foundation.

Traynor, C. (1997) (Personal communication to author).

Twelvetrees, A. C. (1996) *Organizing for Neighbourhood Development: A Comparative Study of Community Based Development Organizations*, 2nd edition, Aldershot, Avebury.

Twelvetrees, A. (1998a) *Community Economic Development: Rhetoric or Reality?*, London, Community Development Foundation.

Twelvetrees, A. (1998b) 'Customised Training in Britain; A Success Story', in A. Twelvetrees (ed.), *Community Economic Development: Rhetoric or Reality?*, London, Community Development Foundation, pp. 175–8.

Twelvetrees, A. (1998c) 'Evaluating the UK Government's Inner Cities Task Force Initiative', in A. Twelvetrees (ed.), *Community Economic Development: Rhetoric or Reality?*, London, Community Development Foundation, pp. 168–74.

Voluntary Activity Unit (1997a) *Measuring Community Development in Northern Ireland: A Handbook for Practitioners*, Belfast, Dept of Health and Social Services.

Voluntary Activity Unit (1997b) *Monitoring and Evaluation of Community Work in Northern Ireland*, Belfast, Dept of Health and Social Services.

Walker, P. (1998) 'A strategic approach to CED', in A. Twelvetrees (ed.), *Community Economic Development: Rhetoric or Reality*, London, Community Development Foundation, pp. 257–63.

Walton, R. E. (1976) 'Two Strategies of Social Change and Their Dilemmas' in F. M. Cox *et al.* (eds), *Strategies of Community Organization*, Illinois, F. E. Peacock.

Welsh Local Government Association (n.d.) *Equal Opportunities and the Modern Local Authority*, Cardiff.

Wilkinson, R. (1996) *Unhealthy Societies: The Afflictions of Inequality*, Routledge.

Willmott, P. (1989) *Community Initiatives: Patterns and Prospects*, London, Policy Studies Institute.

Wilson, D. (1984) *Pressure; The A–Z of Campaigning in Britain*, London, Heinemann.

Index